History of t
Its Engines and Area 51 Testing

By *Jack Wilson*   SBN = 9781724195555

Dedication and Intent

This book is dedicated to Dr. Sue Cunningham, now deceased, who continually asked me to compile some technical info into one place before everyone involved was deceased and it was lost. This book's purpose is for interested individuals, engineers, pilots, students, etc to read about some SR-71 history. This book is intended to answer 95% of all technical questions about the SR-71 and its engines. If I didn't answer your questions, send me an email at: banglyphosate@gmail.com and I will try to answer and include it in the next edition of this book. All info in this book is now **declassified** and the vast majority is already released to the public on the Internet in many various places. Hyperlinks are underlined and are included in this book, for those wanting more information and who have the Internet.

Shown is a SR-71B Trainer Over the Sierra Nevada Mountains in California in 1994. The Raised Second Cockpit is for the Rear Seat Officer. The Dark Patterns on the Wings Is Leaking Fuel and the Red Lines are Warning Lines for Maintenance Personnel to Not Stand Across to Avoid Damaging the Airframe Skin. [1]

General Info About the "Blackbird" and Its Engines – It Stands All Alone Like No Other Plane

Unofficially, the SR-71 carried many nicknames, including the "_Habu_," "_SR_," "_Lady in Black,_" and the "_Sled,_" but most of us know the SR-71 as the "**_Blackbird_**." The <u>SR-71</u> was developed as a long-range strategic reconnaissance aircraft capable of flying at speeds of Mach 3.2 and at 85,000 feet. The first flight of a SR-71 took place on 22 December 1964, at USAF Plant 42 in Palmdale, California, piloted by <u>Bob Gilliland</u>. The SR-71 fleet was retired in 1990, however, the USAF brought some back to service in 1995 and kept several more in operation up until 1998. NASA, at <u>Edwards AFB</u>, California flew the last SR-71 on its final flight in October 1999. [1]

The SR-71 has accumulated many outstanding achievements and has been a total success, based on the fact, that the aircraft still today holds many world records. [2]

The SR-71 Still Holds a Number of Official World Records - Many Over ~40 Years [1]

- ❖ Sustained Speed In Level Flight 7/28/76 - 2,193.16 MPH
- ❖ Sustained Altitude In Level Flight 7/28/76 - 85,069 Feet
- ❖ New York To London 9/1/74 1806.96 MPH - 1 Hour 54 Min 32 Sec (Concorde's record is 2 hours and 52 minutes)
- ❖ London To Los Angeles 9/13/74 1435.59 MPH - 3 Hour 47 Min 39 Sec
- ❖ Kansas City To Washington 3/6/90 2176.08 MPH - 24 Min 58.53 Sec
- ❖ St. Louis To Cincinnati 3/6/90 2189.94 MPH - 8 Min 31.93 Sec

3

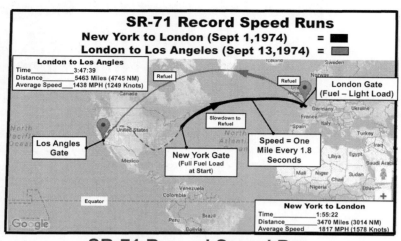

SR-71 Record Speed Runs
New York to London (Sept 1,1974)   = ■
London to Los Angeles (Sept 13,1974) = ▪

London to Los Angles
Time_____3:47:39
Distance_____5463 Miles (4745 NM)
Average Speed___1438 MPH (1249 Knots)

Refuel

Refuel

London Gate
(Fuel – Light Load)

Slowdown to
Refuel

Los Angles
Gate

New York Gate
(Full Fuel Load
at Start)

Speed = One
Mile Every 1.8
Seconds

Equator

New York to London
Time_____1:55:22
Distance_____3470 Miles (3014 NM)
Average Speed___1817 MPH (1578 Knots)

SR-71 Record Speed Run
(Data Courtesy of <u>Lockheed Martin</u> and "*Google Maps*")

The SR-71 refueled before leaving New York and it passed thru the <u>radar timing gates</u> at a high speed with a full load of fuel. It spent one week at the Farnborough International Airshow, with Kelly Johnson - Lockheed's chief designer, before returning. It was not allowed to go supersonic over England. The SR-71 reached the Los <u>Angles return gate</u> before it left London due to the time zone difference as it flew faster than the world turned.

Front View of a *"Blackbird"* [3]

The SR-71 Is Actually Faster Than a Speeding Bullet

The muzzle velocity of a high powered 30-06 hunting rifle is 2938 feet per second with a 165 grain bullet. The "*Blackbird*" flies at 3226 feet per second in cruise (Mach # = 3.2). Of course, that bullet starts to slow down as soon as it leaves the rifle barrel so a SR-71 would certainly win a race. [4] Many SR-71 missions lasted up to ~10 hours (~12,000 nautical miles) however it had to slow down to refuel about 5 to 7 times during that mission (about every 90 minutes). [12]

The "Blackbird" Was Designed and Tested In Secret

The SR-71 plane was tested as a black secret project in Area 51 in Nevada. The plane was designed at Lockheed "*Skunk Works*" in Burbank, California and the engine was designed and tested at a remote site in the Florida Everglades, near Jupiter, Florida.

All "Blackbirds" Are Now Retired

In March of 1990, the 21st production SR-71 aircraft, upon being retired to the National Air and Space Museum in Washington D. C., smashed both the coast-to-coast time and manned speed records. The 1,998-mile flight was flown in a mere 67 minutes and 54 seconds at an average speed of 2,124 MPH. The previous record was held by John Glenn in a FSU Crusader and was shaved by 2 hours and 13 minutes.

Only Rocket Powered Planes Are Faster Than A "Blackbird"

The SR-71 is the fastest and highest flying production manned aircraft in the world. The SR-71 cruises at Mach 3.2 or 2371 MPH. The only aircraft that is faster is an experimental series of X-Planes powered by rocket engines. The X-15 is powered by two rocket engines, which have reached a maximum speed of 4,520 MPH for a short time. This series is launched by a mother ship and the X-15 carried its own oxygen supply.

The fuel for the X-15, a combination of ammonia and liquid oxygen, lasted less than two minutes, and it wasn't a smooth ride. The X-15 went as high as 354,200 feet, around 10 times the cruise altitude of a commercial airliner. The front wheel lacked steering and the main landing gear only had skids (two retractable steel beams that skidded across the landing surface), so a tarmac runway couldn't be used. Instead, the aircraft had to land on a dry lakebed.

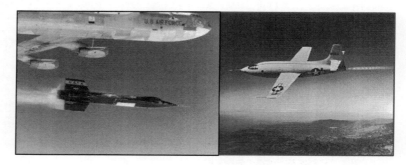

North American Aviation X-15 (Powered by Two Rocket Engine Being Dropped by a B-52 Mother Ship [8]

The Bell X-1 Supersonic Test Plane (Powered by One Rocket Engine) was the First to Break the Sound Barrier on 14 October 1947, Piloted by Chuck Yeager and Launched by a B-29. [9]

The Soviets Started a Competitive Aircraft To The SR-71 But Gave Up Before Finishing

Five R-020 reconnaissance aircraft (Tsybin RSR) were built that should have flown to Mach 3.0 with the Soloviev D-21 turbofan engines, but the engines were not yet ready when Khrushchev cancelled this project in 1961 to funnel the funds into missile development.

Russian R-020 Reconnaissance Aircraft Was Never Finished

The R-020 did fly with ordinary Tumansky R-11F turbojet engines and managed to attain a speed of Mach 2.4 while afterburning. The R-020 might have been a competitive aircraft, but not as fast as the SR-71, had it not been cancelled. It did not carry missiles as the intent was reconnaissance only.

SAM Missile Operators Were Spellbound By The SR-71's

During its operational time, the SR-71 aircraft could literally outfly the enemy's best missiles. If a missile ever came close, a modified J58 engine with extra thrust, including a water-cooled turbine, was designed, tested and available to increase its thrust and aircraft speed. It was never needed and was more complicated due to an extra water tank needed.

The existing J58 engine could reach Mach 3.6 in a SR-71 without exceeding the limits already verified at Pratt and Whitney Aircraft testing facility in Florida. Per the following chart, a SR-71 speed of Mach 3.2 has almost zero chance of being killed by a SA-2 missile with a speed of Mach 3.5.

It stands zero chance if the SR-71 speed is increased the Mach 3.5.

The SR-71 had three <u>cockpit lights</u> - the "*M,*" "*L*" and "*R*" lights. The "*M*" light meant that the enemy had actually fired missiles at you and the "*L*" light meant they were launching at you. The "*R*" light meant they were searching and tracking you.

It is Nearly Impossible for a SAM-2 Missile, With a Speed of Mach of 3.5, To Intercept and Kill a SR-71

The following diagram illustrates why it is nearly impossible for a SAM missile, with a maximum speed of Mach 3.5, to intercept a SR-71 flying at Mach 3.2. The SAM had to launch, accelerate to Mach 3.5, climb, and also track the SR-71.

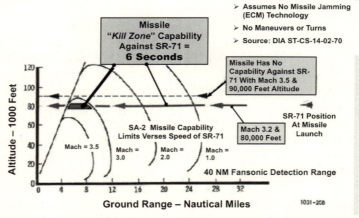

Diagram of <u>SA-2 Missile</u> Against a SR-71 (~6 Second "*Kill Zone*")

The SR-71, with a nominal speed of Mach of 3.2, was simply too fast, with an intercept kill window of only 6 seconds, for a SAM to catch it, ignoring its ability to jam the enemy's missiles and also the ability to maneuver off course. This was enough to make the SAM missile

8

operators cry for fear of being sent to work in the salt mines if not successful, which they never were.

A SAM-2 Missile Was Not Fast Enough To Catch a SR-71

SA-2 Missile on Display

Some pilots, such as Brian Shul and others, estimate that up to 4000 missiles [10] (during the 3,551 mission sorties) were shot at the SR-71 fleet and no SR-71 kill was ever made, although no official records of the missiles shot were kept. [11], [12] & [13]

The Soviet SA-2 missile, which was mostly shot at the SR-71's, had a solid fuel booster rocket that launched and accelerated it, then dropped off after about 4-5 seconds. While in initial boost stage, the missile did not guide, except during the second stage. The SA-2 2nd stage was guided, and the liquid-fuel rocket propelled it for about 22 seconds, to its target. Its maximum range was ~28 miles, with a 288-pound blast-fragmentation warhead, and it weight 4,850 pounds.

The "*Blackbird*" was just too fast, flew too high, and its jamming technology was too sophisticated for a missile to ever catch it.

The SR-71 Also Had Missile Jamming Technology

The SR-71 carried a Deception Repeater System (CFAX-I), one of which is located in the Moffett Museum, Beale Air

9

Force Base, Ca. This technology confused the missile's guidance system and help avoid a SR-71 kill.

Radar Jammer Carried by SR-71

Russian Technology Has Improved Since the 1960's

Russian missile technology has improved since the 1960's. The S-400 missile system, first introduced in 2007, still has a speed of Mach 3.5, weighs 4173 pounds each and has a cost of ~$300 million per system (32 missiles). It is capable of attacking targets at altitudes of 88,500 feet, however, it is still predicted, it could not kill a SR-71.

The latest technology improved <u>S-500</u> missile system, supposedly installed around Moscow in 2021, is capable of a range of ~300 miles and is claimed to attack targets at speeds of Mach 5.0 and 110 miles high, such as satellites. Each system cost ~ $60 million each with a launch response time of 4 seconds. A planned <u>SR-72</u> replacement for the SR-71 is a drone capable of Mach 6.0 and is stealthy and hard to detect.

According to Wikipedia, the latest <u>MIG-31BM</u> aircraft can carry four <u>R-33 missiles</u> under their belly, with a predicted radar detection range, for a SR-71, of 175 miles (282 km). This missile is capable of a speed of Mach 4.5, which could not catch a drone with a speed of Mach 6.0.

The "Blackbird" Variants Consisted of Five Different Planes: <u>(56)</u>

Comparsion Feature	A-12A	YF-12A	SR-71
Service	CIA	USAF & NASA	USAF
Number Built	13	3	32
Length	101 Ft 9 In	101 Ft 9 In	107 Ft 5 In
Wing Span	55 Ft 7 In	55 Ft 7 In	55 Ft 7 In
Max Flight Weight	124,600 Lbs	124,600 Lbs	140,000 lbs
Maximum Speed	Mach = 3.35 2,275 MPH	Mach = 3.35 2,275 MPH	Mach = 3.20 2,176 MPH
Max Test Altitude (Feet)	95,000	90,000	85,000
Range (Miles)	2,500	3,000	3,250
Camera or Armament	Downward Looking	Nuclear Warhead	Side Looking
Crew	One*	Two	Two
* = Two Seats for Trainer Version (One Built)			

SR-71 Verses YF-12A and A-12A <u>(59)</u>
(The A-12 Was 5 Feet- 8 Inches Shorter Than a SR-71)

The A-12 was the first variant of the *"Blackbird"* family. In 1960, the CIA ordered twelve A-12 aircraft. First flown in 1962, it had a short career, and was retired in 1968. The A-12's sat in storage for over twenty years in Palmdale, California before being transported to <u>museums</u> around the country.

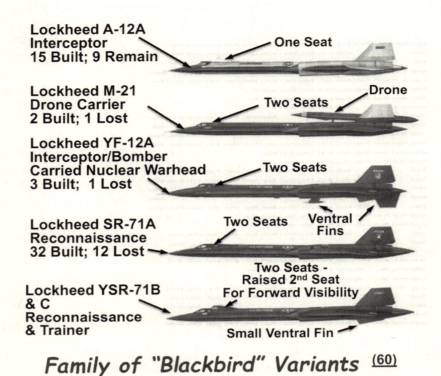

Lockheed A-12A Interceptor 15 Built; 9 Remain — One Seat

Lockheed M-21 Drone Carrier 2 Built; 1 Lost — Two Seats — Drone

Lockheed YF-12A Interceptor/Bomber Carried Nuclear Warhead 3 Built; 1 Lost — Two Seats

Lockheed SR-71A Reconnaissance 32 Built; 12 Lost — Two Seats — Ventral Fins

Lockheed YSR-71B & C Reconnaissance & Trainer — Two Seats - Raised 2nd Seat For Forward Visibility — Small Ventral Fin

Family of "Blackbird" Variants [60]

The A-12 major advantages in capabilities to the SR-71 include a higher-resolution larger camera and its ability to go marginally faster (Mach 3.35) compared to the SR-71 (Mach 3.2).

The SR-71 was chosen as a successor to the A-12 due to its side-looking radar and cameras, allowing it to gather more reconnaissance data without penetrating enemy airspace.

A-12A (*"OXCART"*) [58]
Single Seat Interceptor – "*Blackbird*"

The YF-12A is a prototype for a proposed Mach 3+ A-12 interceptor/bomber. Only three were originally built and only one remains today. The YF-12A carried three AIM-47 missiles (originally called GAR-9), each carrying a 250 kT nuclear warhead in the internal weapons bays behind the cockpit. One of the four bays was filled with electronics and the other three with missiles. Cameras could also replace the missiles. The AIM-47 missile was developed to extend its range to 125 miles from the plane. It had flip-out fins to reduce its diameter and weighed 805 pounds each. Test firings of the AIM-47 from the YF-12's at drones resulted in six kills in seven launches.

The YF-12A took the seventh through ninth slots in the A-12 assembly line at Lockheed. The YF-12A program was cancelled in the mid-1960s for budgetary reasons. However, the aircraft went on to serve NASA before its eventual retirement in 1979.

In order to protect North America, 93 production aircraft needed to be built. However, the YF-12 program was cancelled in the mid-1960s, the Strategic Air Command (SAC) may have felt that the YF-12 would threaten the development of their other supersonic bomber, the XB-70 Valkyrie.

13

YF-12A *"Blackbird"* & AIM - 47 Nuclear Missile
[57] **Interceptor & Nuclear Bomber**

SR-71 *"Blackbird"* [61]
Twin Cockpits - Reconnaissance
(Showing Shock Diamonds).

Nomenclature For the Variants

A-11 was the designation given by Clarence L. (Kelly) Johnson of Lockheed Aircraft Corporation for his initial design study as submitted to the CIA. It was frequently used thereafter, as for example, in the President's announcement and the name was later changed to **A-12**.

A-12 was the official designation of a single-seat version on behalf of "*Spook Central*" (CIA), for a reconnaissance version. It was also the code name for the program, which developed the basic aircraft.

M-21 was a two seat drone carrier, that was cancelled after a crash that killed Ray Torrick - the launch control officer. **D-21** was the secret supersonic reconnaissance drone.

YF-12A was the designation given to a two-seated interceptor version of the A-11, three of which were built for the Air Force. Two of these three were flown to Edwards Air Force Base for display after the President's announcement.

SR-71 became the designation for a two-seated reconnaissance version produced for the Air Force.

SR-71B was a trainer variant and the **SR-71C** was a hybrid trainer aircraft composed of the rear fuselage of the first YF-12A (S/N 60-6934) and the forward fuselage from an SR-71 static test unit. The SR-1B was wrecked in a 1966 landing accident. SR-71C was seemingly not quite straight and had a yaw at supersonic speeds, so it was nicknamed "*The Bastard*." [1]

A total of 12 out of the 32 SR-71 aircraft built were lost. None of the "*Blackbird*"s were lost due to enemy military retaliation. All the SR-71 crew had to do to avoid a kill upon a missile launch, was to increase the throttle and watch the missile get further and further away from striking distance.

The A-12A had one cockpit; the SR-71 had two cockpits; while the YF-12 had two. The A-12A used the extra cockpit area for a larger improved camera and/or missiles.

Following the development of the A-12 came the SR-71, an improved platform designed for reconnaissance. The capabilities of the SR-71 versus the A-12 have been debated many times. Each of these aircraft served different purposes and regardless of which is better, the SR-71 is still a magnificent aircraft. Some sources say that the SR-71 can fly up to 120,000 feet (22.7 miles) but it is officially listed as 85,000 feet (16.1 miles). [1]

SR-71 with 2 Seats (Left) is Similar to the A-12 Single Seat (Right) [62]

A "Blackbird" Derivative Was Used to Launch Drones At High Speed

A drone launch vehicle, the M-21 is an A-12 derivative aircraft designed to launch the once ultra-secret D-21 Drone. Although the M-21 looks like an A-12, it was not modified from one. Development of the M-21 (drone launch vehicle) was called the "*Tagboard*" program.

When the United States signed a treaty to end flights of manned vehicles over the Soviet Union, an unmanned vehicle was needed for reconnaissance. Since the A-12 is an over-flight vehicle, it would undermine this treaty, if used in future overflights.

After the first A-12 prototype (#60-6939) was built, two more M-21's were built for the "*Tagboard*" program. These aircraft had two cockpits: one for a pilot and one for a launch control officer.

In the 1960's, Lockheed's "*Skunk Works*" developed the ultra-secret Mach ~3.5 reconnaissance drone aircraft for the Central Intelligence Agency (CIA), based on the A-12 aircraft.

Drone Vehicle

M-21 "*Blackbird*" Derivative [63]
Two Seater – Drone Launch Vehicle

After some successful launches of D-21 drones, a launch was attempted at Mach 3.25. This risky feat had never been attempted before at this high speed. Aircraft #60-6941 crashed, when the aircraft collided with its D-21 drone during launch, per the chase plane pilot. The M-21 pilot (<u>Bill Park</u>) survived, but the launch control officer (Lockheed employee <u>Ray Torrick</u>) drowned in the Pacific Ocean. It is believed his suit was torn and it filled with water before the rescue helicopter arrived although other theories exist.

After <u>Ray Torrick's</u> suit filled up with water and he downed, this loss drove <u>Kelly Johnson</u> of Lockheed to recommend cancelling of the M-21/D-21 program. The *"Tagboard"* program was cancelled, but later on, two <u>B-52H</u> bombers were modified and were used to launch a number of D-21 drones at a slower speed.

The M-21 accident also prompted water survival training by the A-12 pilots based in Area 51 at <u>Groom Lake</u>. Under the supervision of 1129th SAS commander, <u>Col Hugh Slater</u>, the pilots, wearing their flight suits, lifted high above the waters of Lake Mead on a parasail, towed by a United States Coast

Guard whaler. Colonel Slater quickly aborted the training when some of the fully suited pilots almost drowned after dropping from the parasail into the water.

The remaining M-21 aircraft is on display at the <u>Museum of Flight</u> in Seattle, WA. The engines for the M-21 aircraft were two Improved Pratt & Whitney J58s increased to 40,000 pounds of thrust, from 32,500 pounds.

The D-21 drone engine was a single <u>Marquardt RJ43-MA20-4</u> ramjet with ~1,500 pounds of thrust at 95,000 feet. The drone length was 42.83 feet long and 19.02 feet wide with a weight of ~11,000 pounds. The <u>D-21 drone</u> was fabricated mostly of titanium and carried a 300-pound Hycon HR 335 camera peering through the drone's lower fuselage and could capture 5,600 exposures covering an area 16 miles wide and 3,900 miles long.

<u>Thirty-eight D-21</u> drones were designed and built by Lockheed *"Skunk Works,"* and were capable of speeds in excess of Mach 3.5 and 95,000 feet altitude, with a range of over ~3,000 miles. [64]

D-21 Drone and Its Partial Fleet Designed at *"Skunk Works"* Under Kelly Johnson [65]

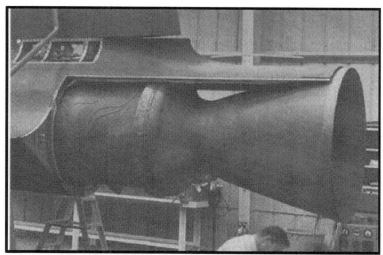

D-21 Drone Engine (Daughter) Being Installed into a M-21 (Mother) [66]

"Blackbirds" Were Also Useful as Research Vehicles

NASA also Used Two YF12A's as Experimental Test-Beds Until Oct 1999. [5]

Experimental Test of a Linear Aerospike Rocket Engine in March 1998. [6]

NASA researchers used the YF-12s for a variety of experiments involving aerodynamic and thermal loads, aerodynamic drag and skin friction, heat transfer, airframe and propulsion system interactions, inlet control system improvements, high-altitude turbulence, boundary-layer flow, landing gear dynamics, measurement of engine effluents for pollution studies, "*Sonic Boom*" noise measurements, and a maintenance monitoring and recording system were also evaluated. On many YF-12 flights, medical researchers obtained information on the physiological and biomedical aspects of crews flying at sustained high speeds. Research data from the YF-12 program also validated analytical theories and wind-tunnel test techniques. [7]

As an example, NASA's tested "*LASRE*" - **L**inear **A**ero**S**pike **R**ocket **En**gine experiment on a "*Blackbird*", which took place, during seven flights, at the Dryden Flight Research Center at Edwards Air Force Base, California.

Exhaust Flow

Linear Aerospike Rocket Engine Experiment Tested on Top of a "*Blackbird*" [6]

This experiment provided flight data to help Lockheed Martin validate and tune the computational predictive tools used to determine the aerodynamic performance of the Lockheed Martin X-33 lifting body and linear Aerospike combination.

The SR-71 Could Outfly Our "Cold War's" Enemies Best Missiles

The only other production aircraft ever to come close to the SR-71's speed, besides the X-15 & X-1, is the Russian MIG-25 "*Foxbat*" and later the MIG-31 "*Foxhound.*" At a sustained speed of more than Mach 3.2, the SR-71 was faster than the Soviet Union's fastest interceptors. The MIG-25 and the MIG-31 could reach speeds of over Mach 3.0 for only a few minutes, before damaging their engines.

During the SR-71 service life, no SR-71 was ever shot down. If its missile detectors alerted on a launch at the SR-71, the standard evasive procedure was to accelerate and outfly the missile. Only once, did a small piece of shrapnel damage a "*Blackbird*" from an exploding missile.

The Soviet Union's Best Interceptors Were Slower Than a SR-71

MIG-25; Speed = Mach 2.83 [13] unless Damage to the Engines is Allowed

MIG-31; Speed = Mach 2.83 [13] unless Damage to the Engines is Allowed

The MIG-31 "*Foxhound*" was designed by the Soviet Mikoyan design bureau as a later replacement for the MIG-25 "*Foxbat*". [14] The MIG-31 shares many of the same features as the MIG-25 and also has a speed of Mach 2.83, the same as MIG-25, for a short period of time. It is comparable to a F-15 Eagle [16] and neither could catch a "*Blackbird,*" which cruises at Mach 3.2 or faster. A cruise missile has a speed of Mach 2.35. [15]

The Max Allowed Speed of a SR-71 Is Mach 3.2, Unless Being Chased By a Missile

The SR-71 flight manual recommended a long-term steady state design speed up to Mach 3.2 (2,371 MPH) under normal conditions. [20] SR-71 pilot Major Brian Shul reported reaching a speed of Mach 3.5 on an operational sortie, while evading a missile over Libya. [1] Other pilots also reported reaching altitudes of 120,000 feet, although the MIG-25 holds the official altitude record of 123,523 feet, set in 1977. [21] The speed and altitude of the SR-71 aircraft simply hypnotized the pilots flying the MIG-31's. [22] It takes about 16 minutes for a MIG-31 pilot to take off after being alerted of an SR-71 flying overhead, which is then too late for a missile to catch it. If it did launch, the missile would not have enough energy to catch the SR-71 and score a kill. No SR-71's were ever shot down by a missile.

The SR-71 Cruises Faster and Higher Than the French Concorde

The French Concorde Is The Only Production Aircraft, Besides The SR-71, That Can Fly At Supersonic Speeds (Mach = 2.04) For Hours at a Time. [159]

The SR-71 service history is as follows: [1]

3,551 Mission Sorties Flown

17,300 Total Sorties Flown

11,008 Mission Flight Hours

53,490 Total Flight Hours

2,752 Hours Mach 3+ Time (Missions)

11,675 Hours Mach 3+ Time (Total)

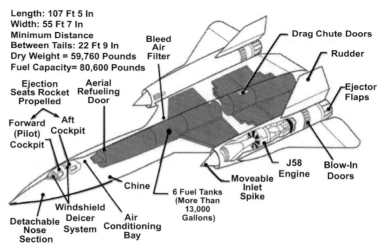

Length: 107 Ft 5 In
Width: 55 Ft 7 In
Minimum Distance
Between Tails: 22 Ft 9 In
Dry Weight = 59,760 Pounds
Fuel Capacity= 80,600 Pounds

General Arrangement of the SR-71 Aircraft
[18] & [19]

The Minimum _Turning Radius_ is Normally 83.5 Nautical Miles

The SR-71 has a minimum turning radius, at 80,000 feet and Mach 3.2, of about 83.5 nautical miles (NM). This is pulling 1.5 g's - the recommended limit is 3g's due to avoiding an "_unstart_" due to the distortion of inlet air. This limitation is due to the wing area with the plane banking 48 degrees. At 80,000 feet, the air is too thin and the wings too small to allow for enough lift to turn sharply. [23]

93% of the SR-71 is Titanium and the Hottest Parts, Including the Chines, Were Helped Cooled with Recycled Fuel

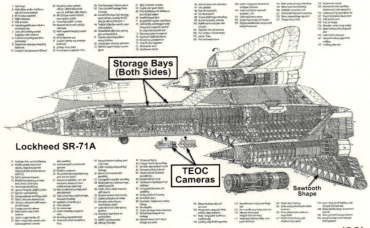

Storage Bays (Both Sides)

Lockheed SR-71A

TEOC Cameras

Sawtooth Shape

SR-71A Cutaway of Airframe (20)

Fuel is used for cooling by cycling the fuel behind the titanium surfaces in front of the wings.

The J58 Engine Was Unique at That Time in History

The Pratt & Whitney J58 is a jet engine used on the CIA's Lockheed A-12 *"OXCART,"* and later the YF-12 and SR-71 *"Blackbird"* aircraft. The J58 is a variable cycle engine, which functioned as both a turbojet and a fan-assisted ramjet. It has one rotor with a variable area afterburner. Bypass jet engines were unique and a first at that time in history. (24) The SR-71 is one of the few aircraft that consumes less fuel as it goes faster.

Each Engine Has The Power of 45 Train Locomotives

Two Pratt and Whitney Aircraft J58 engines power the SR-71 and the Pratt and Whitney designation is JT11D-20. [1] Each engine has 32,500 pounds of thrust (160,000 shaft horsepower), each enough to drive the largest ocean liner (Queen Mary) or more power than 45 train locomotives. During their time of operation, they were the largest of their kind, and also the most powerful in the world. The engine is one part of a propulsion system, which includes an inlet, and an ejector, each producing thrust at cruise speed.

In order for the system to work properly, over a long period of time, the inlet must capture the onrushing air correctly. To do this, a large spike is placed in the inlet and moves forward and back (26 inches total) [25] as conditions change. When the air is not captured properly, an event called an "*unstart*" or stall occurs. An "*unstart*" is best described as a violent yaw where the aircraft pulls to the side with the "*unstart*" engine. To correct the problem, the pilot must push the spike totally forward and adjust it to capture the air properly, which is called a manual intake. Later, an automatic system was developed to adjust the rudder during an "*unstart*" in order to assist the pilot.

The J58 engine operates as an ordinary jet at low speeds, switching to become a ramjet at high speeds above 2,000 MPH.

The SR-71 Was The Ultimate Alpha In A Sky Full Of Alphas - It Cruises in Afterburner Mode for Hours At A Time

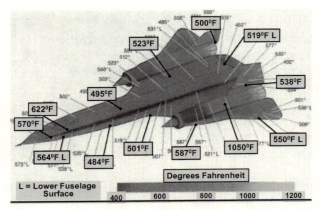

SR-71 Surface Temperatures at Cruise (Mach = 3.2) [2]

You Can Fry an Egg on Its Skin After Landing

Each airframe with its two engines cost <u>$34 million</u> in 1966. [1]

The SR-71 Had to Slow Down Over The Baltic Sea Near <u>Sweden</u>

Whenever the SR-71 made a run north over the Baltic Sea, it would end the run by making a Mach 3 turn westwards, which due to its large turn radius, at that speed, would make it violate Swedish Air Space. Russians detected the SR-71 too late, to be able to intercept. The <u>Swedish Air Force</u> could detect the SR-71 much earlier, as it was passing Southern Sweden and anticipated the violations ~15 minutes in advance. Sweden decided to put a stop to the overflights, using the <u>SAAB JA-37 Viggen</u> aircraft. After the USAF was shown photos, proving that the Viggen could achieve a possible firing solution, the SR-71s slowed down to Mach 2.5 in the Westward turn, allowing them to complete the turn without violating Swedish territory.

The SR-71 Uses Less Fuel Than a Commercial Airliner

The SR-71, at Mach 3.2 and 78,700 feet altitude & 90,000 pounds total weight, flies 54.1 nautical miles per 1000 pounds of fuel. A McDonnell Douglas DC-10, at Mach .84 and 41,000 feet altitude & an average gross weight of its passengers, flies 38.4 nautical miles per 1000 pounds of fuel.

The SR-71 Cruises at 16 Miles High for Hours at a Time

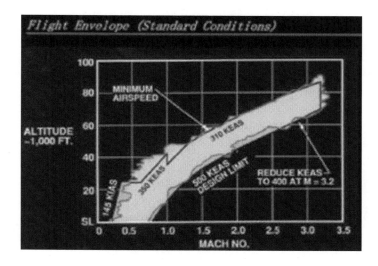

Long Term SR-71 Flight Envelope at Standard Conditions per Lockheed (26) & (27)

The SR-71 was painted black (actually a very dark blue at flight temperatures and speed) to reduce surface temperatures (calculated delta of minus 35 ⁰ F) and it was named *"Blackbird"* accordingly. This low observable paint had to be made fuel-proof as well as rain-proof and it also added an additional 60 pounds. The paint also helps camouflage the plane against the black sky above and also reduces its radar signature. Some pilots called the SR-71 *"Habu"* because it resembled a dangerous venomous pit viper snake.

The "Blackbird" Engines Were Variable Cycle - A First

The engine inlet air is initially compressed and heated by the shock wave cones, and then enters 4 stages of engine compressors. The airflow is then split: some of the air enters the compressor core, while the remaining flow bypasses the core (controlled by variable area actuator) into external ducts to enter the afterburner. The air continuing through the compressor is further compressed before entering the combustor, where it is mixed with fuel and ignited. The temperature reaches its maximum in the combustor, just below the temperature where the cooled turbine blades would soften. The first stage turbine blades are cooled with compressor air. The core air then passes through the turbine and rejoins the bypass air before entering the afterburner.

The main purpose of an inlet cone is to slow the flow of air from supersonic flight speed to a subsonic speed before it enters the engine. At around Mach 3.0, the initial shock-cone compression greatly heats the air, which means that the turbojet portion of the engine must reduce the fuel/air ratio in the combustion chamber so as not to melt the turbine blades. The turbojet components of the engine thus provide less thrust, and the *"Blackbird"* flies with ~80% of its thrust generated by the air that bypassed most of the turbomachinery. The air undergoing combustion in the afterburner portion expands out through the exhaust nozzle, which has variable area.

The Pilots Received Special Meals to Avoid Getting Sick at High Altitude and Reduce Using the Restroom

Before any flight, the crew would receive a high protein, low residue meal of steak and eggs. After that, the crew would have a brief medical examination. Following the examination, the crew would get suited up and the

Physiological Support Division would check the suit integration.

The suits used on the Space Shuttle were later very similar to those that the SR-71 crew members wore, due to the lack of oxygen at high altitude. Their helmets were connected to a hose to supply the needed oxygen. The pilot's suits also protected them from the high heat the SR-71 generated at its high speeds. Inside the cockpit was like a warm oven.

Pilots in Full Pressure & Cooled Suits with a "*Blackbird*" (28)

After the crew is suited up, they breathe in pure oxygen and filter out any other gas from their body before takeoff. The black patches on their suit's legs were "*Velcro*" for the crew to attach an emergency checklist. Then the crew would go out to the van for the trip to the "*Barn*", where the SR-71 is housed. When the crew arrives at the "*Barn*", they shake hands with their buddy backup crew and others before entering the aircraft. A backup crew was always ready in case the primary crew members were unable to fly. After a four-hour mission, a pilot lost an average of five pounds.

A Special Pyrophoric Chemical is Used to Start the SR-71 Engines

The pilot and his rear seat officer enter the aircraft and the pilot will tell the ground crew to start the engines. The pilot will then move up the throttle about half-way up. TEB (Triethylborane) is shot into the combustion chamber of the aircraft and a green flash is seen about 50 feet behind the engine ejector. TEB ignites instantaneously upon contact with air and 16 shots are stored in an inert fuel cooled pressurized tank on top of each engine. The engines are started and then there are about 25 minutes of pre-flight checks before takeoff.

When the aircraft has completed its pre-flight checks, it will pull out of the "*Barn*" and moves onto the runway. From there, the SR-71 will perform engine run-ups and then the ground crew will pull the chocks. The SR-71 has no parking brake, so large chocks must be used instead.

Taking Off In a SR-71 Feels Like Driving a Freight Train Downhill

The SR-71 will start to roll down the runway slowly and then accelerate rather rapidly after the afterburner is lit. The feel has been described as driving a freight train moving down-hill. At approximately 240 MPH, the airplane lifts off the runway.

The main cockpit gauges are analog and has a retractable periscope for the pilot to obtain a rear view and also sun visors to block out the bright sun.

View of the Main Forward Cockpit in a SR-71 [1]

SR-71 Gauges or Switches				
Forward Cockpit			**Rear Cockpit**	
Location	Number		Location	Number
Forward Main Panel	50		Forward Main Panel	34
Forward Side Left & Right Panels	40		Rear Side Left Panel	11
Rear Side Left Panel	27		Rear Side Right Panel	6
Rear Side Right Panel	14		Annuniciator Panel	5
Sub - Total =	131		Total Number =	187

Number of Gauges Per SR-71 Flight Manual [20]

An E6B computer to aid in calculating fuel burn, wind correction, time in route, and other items is also used. The pilots requested an additional device, that was added, in the time frame 1977 thru 1978. It shines a laser beam across the cockpit, which helps with the pilot's orientation to keep the plane level, when desired during refueling. [150]

The pilot can adjust the fuel among the forward and aft fuel tanks to alter the airplane's center of gravity, since it changes as fuel is burned.

Why Was A Razor Blade Mounted on the Instrument Panel?

Even though the pilots wore spacesuits when they flew, Air Force regulations were later revised to also wear an inflatable bladder life vest, when in case they had to eject over water. This was the result from the crash and drowning of a M-21 launch control officer (Lockheed employee Ray Torrick). He drowned in the Pacific Ocean, and it is believed his suit was torn during ejection and it filled with water before the rescue helicopter arrived.

Occasionally, this bladder life vest, due to the cycling pressure changes around the CO_2 cartridge, would accidently inflate. This was quite a hazard to a pilot when flying. As a counter measure, the crew chiefs mounted a single edge razor blade on the instrument panel in a bracket that protected the crew but allowed them to lean into it and deflate the life vest.

These inflated suits later helped save a surviving crew member. The seats and stabilization chutes, as well as the main suits, worked as advertised. The only problem that occurred, on the way down, was icing so the pilot could not see out of his own helmet. The pilot landed on the ground by automation. The seat stabilization system worked perfectly on the way down.

The SR-71 Holds Up to 80,600 Pounds (12,084 Gallons) of JP-7 Fuel and Requires a Dedicated Tanker to Refuel

After the SR-71 takes off, it has a rendezvous with a KC-135Q tanker about seven minutes later. The SR-71 takes off with a very light fuel load, to reduce stress on the tires and brakes, and after this refueling, the plane can fly up to 3,200 miles without refueling. [30] The refueling takes place at nearly the tanker's maximum airspeed (355 Knots Indicated Airspeed).

In-Flight Refueling of a "*Blackbird*" with Dedicated KC-135Q Tanker [31]

The tanker also had a special fuel system for moving JP-4 (for the KC-135Q itself) and JP-7 (for the SR-71) between different tanks.

The longest Blackbird flight was an 11 hour circuit from Griffith Air Force Base in New York to Israel, Egypt, and Syria during the 1973 Yom Kippur War, and required five in-flight refuelings.

Refueling with JP-7 Fuel [32]

The SR-71 Cruises in Afterburner Mode Where No Other Planes Are Flying

After refueling, the pilot lights the afterburners and then the aircraft accelerates to speed and altitude, which is normally about Mach 3.0 to 3.2 and an altitude of 70K feet to 85K feet (>16 miles), and it cruises in the afterburner mode. Operation in continuous afterburner mode is a first for gas turbines. The climb rate for a SR-71 is ~11,820 feet per minute. [1]

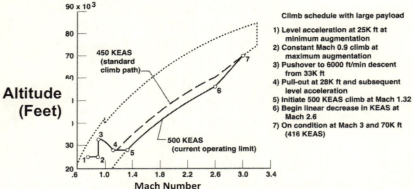

Recommended Climb Schedule [33]

The SR-71 Could _Photograph_ 100,000 Square Miles Per Hour

The SR-71 then takes photos of the targeted area and has another rendezvous with a tanker before returning home. After the flight, the photography equipment is removed and is analyzed immediately. The photography is then sent to the CIA, or whoever needs this valuable intelligence. [30]

A total of 3,551 mission sorties were flown to spy on military installations, troop movements and nuclear silos during the "_Cold War_" with the Soviet Union. The airplane's spy equipment allowed it to survey 100,000 square miles per hour of the Earth's surface from an altitude of 80,000 feet.

The nose and camera bay (behind the cockpits) of the SR-71 carried its cameras. Depending on its mission, multiple cameras were available along with special radar systems.

You Can See The Curvature of the Earth From a SR-71 at 80,000 Feet

Can See Curvature of the Earth.

Can See 350+ Miles.

Black Sky is Overhead and Most (97%) of the Air is Below.

16 Miles Up With No Real Sense of Speed.

Quite Because You Are In a Spacesuit and Supersonic – Noise Is Behind You. So Quite, You Could Hear a Pin Drop.

SR-71 View at 80,000 Feet [34]

Landing a SR-71 and Its Special Tires

Four of the twelve SR-71s that were lost were partially due to <u>tire failure</u> during landings. Three different diameter parachutes are employed in sequence during a single landing to slow down a "*Blackbird.*" Stopping also requires special aluminum-reinforced tires made by B. F. Goodrich, in addition to the brakes. The tires need replacing after about 15 to 20 landings, depending mainly on the amount of fuel carried during landing. When the tires wear down, red chords became visible, signaling a replacement is needed.

Per the SR-71 flight manual, the maximum landing weight is unlimited, however the manual recommends carrying a routine fuel load of 10,000 pounds, for longer tire life. [20] The tires are 22 ply reinforced with powdered aluminum dust mixed into the rubber to help it to withstand a higher heat load and temperature.

The tires are inflated to 415 psi with nitrogen, which reduces the chance of starting a fire during landing due to the absence of oxygen.

The added <u>aluminum</u> causes the tires to be less explosive during landing, caused by increasing temperature due to friction with the runway. Aluminum was mixed in with latex when the tires were created that gives them the very distinct silver color. Each tire cost ~$2300 in 1960 and the SR-71 has eight tires.

The landing gear retracts up into the middle of the fuel tanks, which help reduce the temperature in order to help protect the rubber tires.

Parachutes Were Employed For Landing To Help Slow Down a SR-71 and Reduce Tire Wear

Slowing Down Something That Weighs Up To 140,000 Pounds Is No Joke. [35]

Since the SR-71 lands at ~175 to 200 MPH, it employs three different size drag parachutes in sequence (42 inch diameter, 10 foot diameter, and 40 foot diameter), which reduces the stress in the tires and temperature of the brakes.

Tires Are Inflated to <u>415 PSI</u> with Nitrogen

Tires and Landing Gear Structure for a SR-71
(36)

SR-71 Tires are Limited to 275 MPH Maximum Landing Speed (37)

A small bolt left on the runway would become imbedded into a tire if contact occurred, due to the high loads, therefore the runway would be cleared of any hazardous material before each flight.

Lightening the Load by Dumping Fuel to Reduce Tire, Brake Wear & Improve Safety

Margin

A SR-71 Off-Loading Fuel, at a Rate of About 2,500 Pounds per Minute Before Landing, with a T-38 Chase Plane [5]

The Thermal Growth of a SR-71 is Up to 3.55 Inches at Cruise

The component parts of the "*Blackbird*" fuel system fit loosely together at assembly to allow for thermal expansion at high temperatures. At rest on the ground, a small fuel leak is experienced, counted in drops per minute, since the fuel tank joints in the fuselage only seal at operating temperatures and expansion. There is little danger of a fire since its JP-7 fuel is very stable, with an extremely high flash point, and is extremely difficult to light. A lighted match dropped into the leaking fuel will not start a fire. During the design phase, <u>Kelly Johnson</u>, of Lockheed, offered a $500 award to anyone who could come up with an effective high temperature sealant, which no one collected. Workers and pilots had to be careful since the fuel was slippery. The skin on the inboard wings was also <u>corrugated</u> to prevent buckling due to this thermal growth difference, however it became smooth during flight.

No Effective Fuel Seal Was Found During The Life of the Program

Fuel Leak

Fuel Leaks on the Runway Before Flight [3]

The SR-71 <u>Camera System</u> Could Capture 18"
Wide Buoys Anchored in the Monterey Harbor From 12.3 Miles High

The SR-71 Blackbird carried a wide variety of cameras and sensors. The sensors fall into three basic groups; Optical, Radar, and Elint (Gathering of electronic intelligence by electronic means). There were on-going modifications and updates to the cameras as capabilities improved and camera resolutions increased. There was initially an Infrared system installed for several years at the beginning of the operational missions, but it was discarded around 1970. The nose and camera bay of the SR-71 carried various cameras depending on its particular mission. [38] The <u>TEOC cameras</u> were mounted in a fuselage bay behind the cockpits, while the optical bar camera was mounted in an especially fabricated detachable nose. [46]

Perkin-Elmer provided the original lenses for the camera systems used in the U-2 and the SR-71 *"Blackbird"* spy planes including huge 36 inch f/4.0 lenses weighing ~200 pounds. James Baker designed the camera and lenses for Perkin-Elmer used on the U-2 spy plane and later the SR-71 *"Blackbird."*

Original Perkin-Elmer Camera with 36 Inch Lens [39]

The Perkin-Elmer (P-E) entry, known as the Type-1 camera, was a high-ground-resolution general stereo camera with 6.6-inch film width size. It produced pairs of photographs covering a swath 71 miles wide with an approximately 30-percent stereo overlap. This system initially had a 5,000-foot film length supply and was able to resolve 140 lines in a single millimeter. [38]

Later Camera Designs (Optical Bar Camera) Carried a Spool of Film Up to Two Miles Long [41] & [42]

ITEK Corporation is a defense contractor that initially specialized in camera systems for use in the **U-2**, SR-71 aircraft, and later spy **satellites.** ITEK called their camera version the Optical Bar Camera (OBC). These were first used in the 1960s and all of the satellites came to use their rotating panoramic camera, which are still in use today. The cameras on the SR-71 could capture the image of 18" wide buoys anchored in the Monterey Harbor at 12.3 miles high. [43]

This photo is taken from 65,000 feet (12.3 miles) above the Monterey Harbor in California. [160]

The **Optical Bar Camera** produced by ITEK, and also used in other aircraft like the U-2 Dragon Lady, the A-12 and **satellites**. Part of the nose cone designed for this camera had a glass quartz strip on the underside of the nose cone that allowed the camera to look below to take photos.

The optical bar camera (OBC) took photographs, while scanning from left to right across the SR-71's flight path. The OBC's terrain coverage was ~2 nautical miles along the ground track and extended ~36 nautical miles to each side of the aircraft (further if banked). Sufficient film was onboard to cover approximately 2,952 NM, or 1,476 NM in stereo mode. [45]

SR-71 Sensors, Cameras, Mission Equipment, Etc

ASARS (Advanced Synthetic Aperture Radar System)

SR-71 With Its Variety of Sensors, Cameras and Mission Equipment [40]

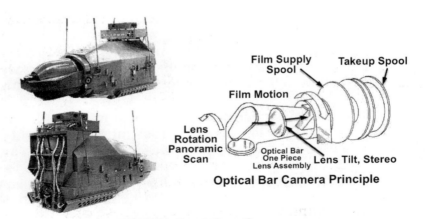

Film Supply Spool

Takeup Spool

Film Motion

Lens Rotation Panoramic Scan

Optical Bar One Piece Lens Assembly

Lens Tilt, Stereo

Optical Bar Camera Principle

ITEK Optical Bar Camera

Later ITEK Optical Bar Camera for the SR-71
(44)

ITEK's Camera Could Photograph Ten States In One Flight

The Optical Bar Camera could survey Florida, Georgia, Alabama, Louisiana, South Carolina, North Carolina, Tennessee, Maryland, Virginia, West Virginia all in a four-hour time frame.

The TEOC Camera Has a Six Inch Focal Length and High Image Resolution

The technical objective camera (TEOC) was made by Fairchild and has a six-inch focal length lens with 9 inch wide film. Each SR-71 was equipped with two of these for stereo resolution.

<u>Image resolution</u> is basically the amount of detail an image can show. It is the quantification of the degree to which two lines next to each other can be visibly resolved, or discerned from each other. If a camera, film or lens can produce an image where you can see clearly defined edges of the smallest details, the resolution is said to be high.

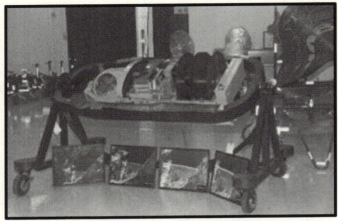

TEOC Camera [47]

Three Different Nose Section Designs with Its Own "R2-D2"

The nose is held to the main fuselage with four large bolts and can be replaced in a little less than two hours. The SR-71 carries ~4,600 pounds of mission equipment. [48] Items such as cameras, radar jamming equipment, sensors, antennas, navigation equipment and other sensors.

<u>Navigation</u> Unit Used on SR-71

The navigation system was an early version of GPS, except it locked to the stars instead of satellites and it was given the nickname "*R2-D2*". [49]

Columbus Used The Same Stars To Navigate As The SR-71

The navigation system provides proof of the SR-71 flight path if the enemy accused us of flying over their territory. It is amazing that Columbus used the same stars to navigate as the SR-71.

The Nose of a SR-71 is Held to the Nose Fuselage with Four Large Bolts.

Three different nose sections are available with various configurations depending on the mission. One is for training purposes while two are configured for missions – with radar and cameras.

Nose Configurations with Radar [50] & [51]

One of the First Planes Designed with a Reduced Radar Cross Section – 10% of a F15 Eagle

The SR-71 was the one of the first early attempts at stealth technology. The shape of the SR-71 was based on that of the A-12, which was the first aircraft to be designed with a reduced radar cross-section. The overall platform was designed to deflect radar waves, but there were several other physical additions to help improve its radar signature. These included spiked cones to shield the face of the inlets for the plane's two J58 engines, chines on the outside of the engine nacelles and engine ducts, curved extensions on the leading edges of the wings, and specially canted rear vertical rudders, made of a composite material to reduce the radar signature. Below the surface of its chinned leading edges, radar defeating saw-tooth baffles also helped deaden the aircraft's radar returns. These qualities gave a very short time for an enemy surface-to-air missile (SAM) site to acquire and track the aircraft although radar could still detect a SR-71. (52)

The paint of a SR-71 is iron base radar absorbing containing tiny spheres of iron and also laced with non-fibrous asbestos (not a bad name in 1960s). Lockheed developed this special "*iron paint*," sometimes referred to as the "*iron ball paint*" because the mixture contained tiny iron balls, to help absorb radar waves. The special blend, which was applied to the SR-71, reportedly cost $400 per quart in the 1960s. (52)

"Plasma Stealth" Was Used on the A-12 and SR-71 to Reduce Its Signature

Fuel is JP-7 with a Cesium containing compound known as A-50, which is to aid in disguising the radar and infrared signatures of the exhaust plume. (53) Lockheed nicknamed it "*Panther Piss*." A-50 was 30 percent Cesium metal and 60 percent Dialkyl Phosphate. It reduces the radar signature of the plane's engine exhausts and afterburner plumes by creating an ionizing cloud behind the aircraft to help conceal its entire rear aspect from radar waves. [52]

JP-7 is unusual, in that it is not a conventional distillate fuel, but is created from special blending stocks in order to have very low (<3%) concentration of highly volatile components like benzene or toluene, and almost no sulfur, oxygen, and nitrogen impurities. It has a low vapor pressure, and high thermal oxidation stability.

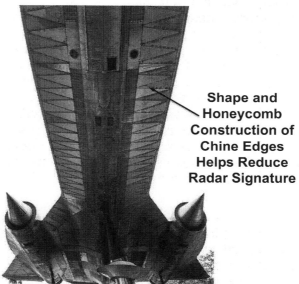

Shape and Honeycomb Construction of Chine Edges Helps Reduce Radar Signature

Fuel Assisted Cooled Chines with Radar Absorbing Edges and Shape Were Incorporated To Reduce Its RCS

The "*Blackbird*" was originally not going to have chines, but they were added to reduce the radar cross section. The SR-71 was based on early studies in radar stealth (RCS) technology, which indicated that a shape with flattened, tapering sides would reflect the most energy away from a radar beam's place of origin. The chine edges are radar absorbing honeycomb composite structure fabricated in a triangular interlocking "*sawtooth*" shape.

Electron Guns Were Developed That Created Radar Absorbing Fields

Powerful electron guns were developed that the A-12 would carry inside its fuselage created radar-absorbing fields. [161]

Canted Vertical Rudders Were a First

The special canted rear vertical rudders were made of composite radar absorbing material, a first for a major airframe part. The vertical tail surfaces were canted inward 15^0 to provide less reflection of radar waves.

Composite Rudders are Canted 15^0 Inward

Tilted Rudders Made of Composite Material Reduced the Radar Cross Section

The SR-71 had a radar cross-section (RCS) of around 110 Square Feet. Engineers had added chines and canted the vertical control surfaces to reduce its radar signature.

The radar signature is about the size of a small J-3 Piper Cub or about one tenth that of a F-15 Eagle. [1] Designed twenty-five years later, the B 1- bomber resulted in a larger radar signature than the SR-71.

Artist Rendering of the Radar Tests, on a Telescoping Pole with a Full Size Model, is Available at Groom Lake, Nevada [54]

Titanium Was Smuggled From Russia to Build The SR-71, However the Russians Never Had an Inkling [1]

Titanium was in short supply in the United States, so the *"Skunk Works"* team was forced to look elsewhere for the metal. Much of the needed material came from the Soviet Union. Colonel Rich Graham, SR-71 pilot, described the acquisition process:

"The airplane is ~93% titanium inside and out. Back when they were building the airplane, the United States didn't have the ore supplies - an ore called rutile ore. It's a very sandy soil and it's only found in very few parts of the world. The major supplier of the ore was the USSR. Working through Third World countries and bogus dummy company operations, they were able to get the rutile ore shipped to the United States to build the SR-71, from the completely oblivious Soviet Union". [1]

Sled Driver - Flying the World's Fastest Jet"
By SR-71 Pilot <u>Brian Shul</u> ⁽⁵⁵⁾

(Book is Limited Print Version & Out of Print)

About Brian Shul – Brian was flying a T-28 aircraft when he was shot down over Vietnam. He was badly burned and spent over a year in the hospital with 15 operations. He overcame this to pilot the SR-71, while taking some stunning photos, that only a pilot and amateur photographer could take.

Excerpt From "Sled Driver" Book

"There were a lot of things we couldn't do in an SR-71, but we were the fastest guys on the block and loved reminding our fellow aviators of this fact. People often asked us if, because of this fact, it was fun to fly the jet. Fun would not be the first word I would use to describe flying this plane. Intense, maybe even cerebral. But there was one day in our Sled experience when we would have to say that it was pure fun to be the fastest guys out there, at least for a moment.

It occurred when Walt and I were flying our final training sortie. We needed 100 hours in the jet to complete our training and attain Mission Ready status. Somewhere over Colorado we had passed the century mark. We had made the turn in Arizona and the jet was performing flawlessly. My gauges were wired in the front seat and we were starting to feel pretty good about ourselves, not only because we would soon be flying real missions but because we had gained a great deal of confidence in the plane in the past ten months. Ripping across the barren deserts 80,000 feet below us, I could already see the coast of California from the Arizona border. I was, finally, after many humbling months of simulators and study, ahead of the jet.

I was beginning to feel a bit sorry for Walter in the back seat. There he was, with no really good view of the incredible sights before us and tasked with monitoring four different radios. This was good practice for him for when we began flying real missions and when a priority transmission from headquarters could be vital. It had been difficult, too, for me to relinquish control of the radios, as during my entire flying career I had controlled my own transmissions. But it was part of the division of duties in this plane and I had adjusted to it. I still insisted on talking on the radio while we were on the ground, however. Walt was so good at many things, but he couldn't match my expertise at sounding smooth on the radios, a skill that had been honed sharply with years in fighter squadrons where the slightest radio miscue was grounds for beheading. He understood that and allowed me that luxury. Just to get a sense of what Walt had to contend with, I pulled the radio toggle switches and monitored the frequencies along with him. The predominant radio chatter was from Los Angeles Center, far below us, controlling daily traffic in their sector. While they had us on their scope (albeit briefly), we were in uncontrolled airspace and normally would not talk to them unless we needed to descend into their airspace.

We listened as the shaky voice of a lone Cessna pilot who asked Center for a read-out of his ground speed. Center replied: "November Charlie 175, I'm showing you at ninety knots on the ground." Now the thing to understand about Center controllers was that whether they were talking to a rookie pilot in a Cessna, or to Air Force One, they always spoke in the exact same, calm, deep, professional tone that made one feel important. I referred to it as the "Houston Center voice." I have always felt that after years of seeing documentaries on this country's space program and *listening to the calm and distinct voice of the Houston controllers, that all other controllers since then wanted to sound like that and that they basically did. And it didn't matter what sector of the country we would be flying in, it always seemed like the same guy was talking. Over the years that tone of voice had become somewhat of a comforting sound to pilots everywhere. Conversely, over the years, pilots always wanted to ensure that, when transmitting, they sounded like Chuck Yeager, or at least like John Wayne. Better to die than sound bad on the radios.*

Just moments after the Cessna's inquiry, a Twin Beech piped up on frequency, in a rather superior tone, asking for his ground speed in the Beech. "I have you at one hundred and twenty-five knots of ground speed." Boy, I thought, the Beechcraft really must think he is dazzling his Cessna brethren.

Then out of the blue, a Navy F-18 pilot out of NAS Lemoore came up on frequency. You knew right away it was a Navy jock because he sounded very cool on the radios. "Center, Dusty 52 ground speed check." Before Center could reply, I'm thinking to myself, hey, Dusty 52 has a ground speed indicator in that million-dollar cockpit, so why is he asking Center for a read-out? Then I got it, ol' Dusty here is making sure that every bug smasher from Mount Whitney to the Mojave knows what true speed is. He's the fastest dude in the valley today, and he just wants everyone to know how much fun he is having in his new Hornet. And the reply, always with that same, calm, voice, with more distinct alliteration than emotion: "Dusty 52, Center, we have you at 620 on the ground." And I thought to myself, is this a ripe situation, or what? As my hand instinctively reached for the mic button, I had to remind myself that Walt was in control of the radios. Still, I thought, it must be done in mere seconds we'll be out of the sector and the opportunity will be lost. That Hornet must die, and die now. I thought about all of our SIM training and how important it was that we developed well as a crew and knew that to jump in on the radios now would destroy the integrity of all that we had worked toward becoming. I was torn.

Somewhere, 13 miles above Arizona, there was a pilot screaming inside his space helmet. Then, I heard it the click of the mic button from the back seat. That was the very moment that I knew Walter and I had become a crew. Very professionally, and with no emotion, Walter spoke: "Los Angeles Center, Aspen 20, can you give us a ground speed check?" There was no hesitation, and the reply came as if it was an everyday request.

"**Aspen 20, I show you at one thousand eight hundred and forty-two knots, across the ground.**" I think it was the forty-two knots that I liked the best, so accurate and proud was Center to deliver that information without hesitation, and you just knew he was smiling. But the precise point at which I knew that Walt and I were going to be really good friends for a long time was when he keyed the mic once again to say, in his most fighter-pilot-like voice: "**Ah, Center, much thanks, we're showing closer to nineteen hundred on the money.**"

For a moment Walter was a god. And we finally heard a little crack in the armor of the Houston Center voice when L.A. came back with, "**Roger that Aspen. Your equipment is probably more accurate than ours. You boys have a good one.**" It all had lasted for just moments, but in that short, memorable sprint across the southwest the Navy had been flamed, all mortal airplanes on frequency were forced to bow before the King of Speed, and more importantly, Walter and I had crossed the threshold of being a crew. A fine day's work. We never heard another transmission on that frequency all the way to the coast. For just one day, it truly was fun being the fastest guys out there."

Bill Weaver's SR-71 Disintegration Story on an Experimental Evaluation Flight
(By Bill Weaver)

Bill Weaver was a *"Skunk Works"* test pilot and has flight tested all models of the Mach 2 F-104 *"Starfighter"* and the entire family of Mach 3+ *"Blackbirds"* - the A-12, YF-12 and SR-71. After the SR-71 disintegration, he became the company's chief pilot and retired as Division Manager of Commercial Flying Operations. He went on to fly Orbital Sciences Corp.'s L-1011, which has been modified to carry a Pegasus satellite-launch vehicle.

"By far, the most memorable flight occurred on Jan. 25, 1966. Jim Zwayer, a Lockheed flight test reconnaissance, and navigation systems specialist, and I were evaluating those systems on an SR-71 Blackbird test from Edwards AFB, Calif. We also were investigating procedures designed to reduce trim drag and improve high-Mach cruise performance. The latter involved flying with the center-of-gravity (CG) located further aft than normal, which reduced the Blackbird's longitudinal stability.

We took off from Edwards at 11:20 a.m. and completed the mission's first leg without incident. After refueling from a KC-135 tanker, we turned eastbound, accelerated to a Mach 3.2-cruise speed and climbed to 78,000 ft., our initial cruise-climb altitude.

Several minutes into cruise, the right engine inlet's automatic control system malfunctioned, requiring a switch to manual control. The SR-71's inlet configuration was automatically adjusted during supersonic flight to decelerate air flow in the duct, slowing it to subsonic speed before reaching the engine's face. This was accomplished by the inlet's center-body spike translating aft, and by modulating the inlet's forward bypass doors. Normally, these actions were scheduled automatically as a function of Mach number, positioning the normal shock wave (where air flow becomes subsonic) inside the inlet to ensure optimum engine performance.

Without proper scheduling, disturbances inside the inlet could result in the shock wave being expelled forward--a phenomenon known as an "inlet unstart." That causes an instantaneous loss of engine thrust, explosive banging noises and violent yawing of the aircraft--like being in a train wreck. Unstarts were not uncommon at that time in the SR-71's development, but a properly functioning system would recapture the shock wave and restore normal operation.

On the planned test profile, we entered a programmed 35-deg. bank turn to the right. An immediate "unstart" occurred on the right engine, forcing the aircraft to roll further right and start to pitch up. I jammed the control stick as far left and forward as it would go. No response. I instantly knew we were in for a wild ride.

I attempted to tell Jim what was happening and to stay with the airplane until we reached a lower speed and altitude. I didn't think the chances of surviving an ejection at Mach 3.18 and 78,800 ft. were very good. However, g-forces built up so rapidly that my words came out garbled and unintelligible, as confirmed later by the cockpit voice recorder.

The cumulative effects of system malfunctions, reduced longitudinal stability, increased angle-of-attack in the turn, supersonic speed, high altitude and other factors imposed forces on the airframe that exceeded flight control authority and the Stability Augmentation System's ability to restore control.

Everything seemed to unfold in slow motion. I learned later the time from event onset to catastrophic departure from controlled flight was only 2-3 sec. Still trying to communicate with Jim, I blacked out, succumbing to extremely high g-forces. The SR-71 then literally disintegrated around us. From that point, I was just along for the ride.

My next recollection was a hazy thought that I was having a bad dream. Maybe I'll wake up and get out of this mess, I mused. Gradually regaining consciousness, I realized this was no dream; it had really happened. That also was disturbing, because I could not have survived what had just happened. Therefore, I must be dead. Since I didn't feel bad--just a detached sense of euphoria--I decided being dead wasn't so bad after all. AS FULL AWARENESS took hold, I realized I was not dead, but had somehow separated from the airplane. I had no idea how this could have happened; I hadn't initiated an ejection. The sound of rushing air and what sounded like straps flapping in the wind confirmed I was falling, but I couldn't see anything. My pressure suit's face plate had frozen over and I was staring at a layer of ice.

The pressure suit was inflated, so I knew an emergency oxygen cylinder in the seat kit attached to my parachute harness was functioning. It not only supplied breathing oxygen, but also pressurized the suit, preventing my blood from boiling at extremely high altitudes. I didn't appreciate it at the time, but the suit's pressurization had also provided physical protection from intense buffeting and g-forces. That inflated suit had become my own escape capsule.

My next concern was about stability and tumbling. Air density at high altitude is insufficient to resist a body's tumbling motions, and centrifugal forces high enough to cause physical injury could develop quickly. For that reason, the SR-71's parachute system was designed to automatically deploy a small-diameter stabilizing chute shortly after ejection and seat separation. Since I had not intentionally activated the ejection system--and assuming all automatic functions depended on a proper ejection sequence--it occurred to me the stabilizing chute may not have deployed.

However, I quickly determined I was falling vertically and not tumbling. The little chute must have deployed and was doing its job. Next concern: the main parachute, which was designed to open automatically at 15,000 feet. Again I had no assurance the automatic-opening function would work. I couldn't ascertain my altitude because I still couldn't see through the iced-up face plate. There was no way to know how long I had been blacked-out or how far I had fallen. I felt for the manual-activation D-ring on my chute harness, but with the suit inflated and my hands numbed by cold, I couldn't locate it. I decided I'd better open the face plate, try to estimate my height above the ground, then locate that "D" ring. Just as I reached for the face plate, I felt the reassuring sudden deceleration of main-chute deployment. I raised the frozen face plate and discovered its uplatch was broken. Using one hand to hold that plate up, I saw I was descending through a clear, winter sky with unlimited visibility. I was greatly relieved to see Jim's parachute coming down about a quarter of a mile away. I didn't think either of us could have survived the aircraft's breakup, so seeing Jim had also escaped lifted my spirits incredibly. I could also see burning wreckage on the ground a few miles from where we would land. The terrain didn't look at all inviting - a desolate, high plateau dotted with patches of snow and no signs of habitation. I tried to rotate the parachute and look in other directions. But with one hand devoted to keeping the face plate up and both hands numb from high-altitude, subfreezing temperatures, I couldn't manipulate the risers enough to turn. Before the breakup, we'd started a turn in the New Mexico-Colorado-Oklahoma-Texas border region. The SR-71 had a turning radius of about 100 mi. at that speed and altitude, so I wasn't even sure what state we were going to land in. But, because it was about 3:00 p.m., I was certain we would be spending the night out here.

At about 300 feet above the ground, I yanked the seat kit's release handle and made sure it was still tied to me by a long lanyard. Releasing the heavy kit ensured I wouldn't land with it attached to my derriere, which could break a leg or cause other injuries. I then tried to recall what survival items were in that kit, as well as techniques I had been taught in survival training.

Looking down, I was startled to see a fairly large animal--perhaps an antelope--directly under me. Evidently, it was just as startled as I was because it literally took off in a cloud of dust.

My first-ever parachute landing was pretty smooth. I landed on fairly soft ground, managing to avoid rocks, cacti and antelopes. My chute was still billowing in the wind, though.

57

I struggled to collapse it with one hand, holding the still-frozen face plate up with the other.

"Can I help you?" a voice said. Was I hearing things? I must be hallucinating. Then I looked up and saw a guy walking toward me, wearing a cowboy hat. A helicopter was idling a short distance behind him. If I had been at Edwards and told the search-and-rescue unit that I was going to bail out over the Rogers Dry Lake at a particular time of day, a crew couldn't have gotten to me as fast as that cowbo-pilot had.

The gentleman was Albert Mitchell, Jr., owner of a huge cattle ranch in northeastern New Mexico. I had landed about 1.5 miles from his ranch house - and from a hangar for his two-place Hughes helicopter. Amazed to see him, I replied I was having a little trouble with my chute. He walked over and collapsed the canopy, anchoring it with several rocks. He had seen Jim and me floating down and had radioed the New Mexico Highway Patrol, the Air Force and the nearest hospital.

Extracting myself from the parachute harness, I discovered the source of those flapping-strap noises heard on the way down. My seat belt and shoulder harness were still draped around me, attached and latched. The lap belt had been shredded on each side of my hips, where the straps had fed through knurled adjustment rollers. The shoulder harness had shredded in a similar manner across my back. The ejection seat had never left the airplane; I had been ripped out of it by the extreme forces, seat belt and shoulder harness still fastened.

I also noted that one of the two lines that supplied oxygen to my pressure suit had come loose, and the other was barely hanging on. If that second line had become detached at high altitude, the deflated pressure suit wouldn't have provided any protection. I knew an oxygen supply was critical for breathing and suit-pressurization but didn't appreciate how much physical protection an inflated pressure suit could provide. That the suit could withstand forces sufficient to disintegrate an airplane and

58

shred heavy nylon seat belts yet leave me with only a few bruises and minor whiplash was impressive. I truly appreciated having my own little escape capsule. After helping me with the chute, Mitchell said he'd check on Jim. He climbed into his helicopter, flew a short distance away and returned about 10 min. later with devastating news: Jim was dead. Apparently, he had suffered a broken neck during the aircraft's disintegration and was killed instantly. Mitchell said his ranch foreman would soon arrive to watch over Jim's body until the authorities arrived.

I asked to see Jim and, after verifying there was nothing more that could be done, agreed to let Mitchell fly me to the Tucumcari hospital, about 60 mi. to the south.

I have vivid memories of that helicopter flight, as well. I didn't know much about rotorcraft, but I knew a lot about "red lines," and Mitchell kept the airspeed at or above red line all the way. The little helicopter vibrated and shook a lot more than I thought it should have. I tried to reassure the cowboy-pilot I was feeling OK; there was no need to rush. But since he'd notified the hospital staff that we were inbound, he insisted we get there as soon as possible. I couldn't help but think how ironic it would be to have survived one disaster only to be done in by the helicopter that had come to my rescue.

However, we made it to the hospital safely--and quickly. Soon, I was able to contact Lockheed's flight test office at Edwards. The test team there had been notified initially about the loss of radio and radar contact, then told the aircraft had been lost. They also knew what our flight conditions had been at the time, and assumed no one could have survived. I briefly explained what had happened, describing in fairly accurate detail the flight conditions prior to breakup.

The next day, our flight profile was duplicated on the SR-71 flight simulator at Beale AFB, Calif. The outcome was identical. Steps were immediately taken to prevent a recurrence of our accident. Testing at a CG aft of normal limits was discontinued, and trim-drag issues were

59

subsequently resolved via aerodynamic means. The inlet control system was continuously improved and, with subsequent development of the Digital Automatic Flight and Inlet Control System, inlet unstarts became rare. Investigation of our accident revealed that the nose section of the aircraft had broken off aft of the rear cockpit and crashed about 10 mi. from the main wreckage. Parts were scattered over an area approximately 15 mi. long and 10 mi. wide. Extremely high air loads and g-forces, both positive and negative, had literally ripped Jim and me from the airplane. Unbelievably good luck is the only explanation for my escaping relatively unscathed from that disintegrating aircraft.

Two weeks after the accident, I was back in an SR-71, flying the first sortie on a brand-new bird at Lockheed's Palmdale, Calif., assembly and test facility. It was my first flight since the accident, so a flight test engineer in the back seat was probably a little apprehensive about my state of mind and confidence. As we roared down the runway and lifted off, I heard an anxious voice over the intercom. "Bill! Bill! Are you there?"

"Yeah, George. What's the matter?"

"Thank God! I thought you might have left." The rear cockpit of the SR-71 has no forward visibility--only a small window on each side--and George couldn't see me. A big red light on the master-warning panel in the rear cockpit had illuminated just as we rotated, stating, "Pilot Ejected." Fortunately, the cause was a misadjusted microswitch, not my departure."

A 2 Inch Long Piece of Duct Tape Caused the Crash of Blackbird # 953

SR-71 #953 fell apart in midair and crashed on the ground east of Death Valley near the village of Shoshone, California. After 7 weeks into a detailed investigation, the Safety Board found the evidence that caused #953 to go down...a piece of tape rolled into cigarette shape made into a well-meaning plug to keep dust and shavings from entering into the pitot-static tube. This duct tape found inside the tube that normally provides dynamic and static pressures for the flight instruments. It was assumed to be forgotten and unseen, since it was hidden inside the tube. The pilot and co-pilot ejected safely.

Crash of "*Blackbird*" # 953

Early Study For The Replacement Of The U2 - "Suntan" Program" with Liquid Hydrogen Fuel

"*Suntan*" was the code-name of a prototype reconnaissance secret aircraft program, with the goal of creating a much faster and higher-altitude successor to the U-2, enabled by the use of liquid hydrogen as aircraft fuel. The program was started in 1956 and cancelled in 1958. The U-2 was shot down by the Soviets in May 1960, so the prediction that a replacement was needed was correct.

The United States Air Force funded a highly secretive program of research and development on high-speed aircraft for long-range reconnaissance. Lockheed's "*Skunk Works*" was the natural partner for this work, having successfully delivered the U-2 and having all the required secrecy and security arrangements to keep the program secret.

Lockheed settled on the CL- 400 design, which looked like a greatly scaled-up Lockheed F-104 Starfighter. The main change to the layout were the twin engines, mounted on the wing tips. Liquid hydrogen was the fuel of choice due to its predictable burning characteristics and the fuel's light weight, although the low density required a large fuselage to hold all of the required fuel.

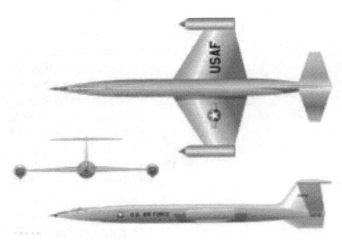

Lockheed CL- 400 Design For The "*Suntan*" Hydrogen Fuel Program [(162)]

Program successes included the concept design of a Mach 2.5 aircraft capable of flying at 98,000 feet and Pratt's successful conversion of an existing turbojet engine to run on liquid hydrogen called the 304 engine. Engine tests began on 11 September 1957 and the engine was tested ~25+ hours with liquid hydrogen as the fuel. Techniques for handling liquid hydrogen on the ground, including making the fuel, transporting and rapid refueling systems, were all developed as part of the "*Suntan*" program.

Budgetary pressures, plus the fact that a hydrogen-powered aircraft was considered too dangerous and expensive to maintain, led to the project's cancellation. In addition, hydrogen fuel would have meant that existing airbases would have needed extensive facilities to handle the aircraft.

The existence of the CL-400 was not fully disclosed to the public until the 1970s, when Lockheed discussed the possibility of using hydrogen as an alternative fuel for future aircraft.

The "Oxcart" Story
Courtesy of Thomas P. McIninch of the CIA [67]

One spring day in 1962 a test pilot named Louis Schalk, employed by the Lockheed Aircraft Corporation, took off from the Nevada desert in an aircraft the like of which had never been seen before. A casual observer would have been startled by the appearance of this vehicle; he would perhaps have noticed especially its extremely long, slim, shape, its two enormous jet engines, its long, sharp, projecting nose, and its swept-back wings, which appeared far too short to support the fuselage in flight. He might well have realized that this was a revolutionary airplane; he could not have known that it would be able to fly at three times the speed of sound for more than 3,000 miles without refueling, or that toward the end of its flight, when fuel began to run low, it could cruise at over 90,000 feet. Still less would he have known of the equipment it was to carry, or of the formidable problems attending its design and construction.

There was, of course, no casual observer present. The aircraft had been designed and built for reconnaissance; it was projected as a successor to the U-2. Its development had been carried out in profound secrecy. Despite the numerous designers, engineers, skilled and unskilled workers, administrators, and others who had been involved in the affair, no authentic accounts, and indeed scarcely any accounts at all, had leaked. Many aspects have not been revealed to this day, and many are likely to remain classified for some time to come.

The official designation of the aircraft was A-12. By a sort of inspired perversity, however, it came to be called, a code word also applied to the program under which it was developed. The secrecy in which it was so long shrouded has lifted a bit, and the purpose of this article is to give some account of the inception, development, operation, and untimely demise of this remarkable airplane. The plane no longer flies, but it left a legacy of technological achievement, which points the way to new projects. And it became the progenitor of a similar but somewhat less sophisticated reconnaissance vehicle called the SR-71, whose existence is well known to press and public.

Sequel to the U-2

The U-2 is dated from 1954, when its development began under the direction of a group headed by Richard M. Bissell of CIA. In June 1956, the aircraft became operational, but officials predicted that its useful lifetime over the USSR could hardly be much more than 18 months or two years. Its first flights over Soviet territory revealed that the air defense warning system not only detected but tracked it quite accurately. Yet it remained a unique and invaluable source of intelligence information for almost four years, until on 1 May 1960, Francis Gary Powers was shot down near Sverdlovsk, Russia.

Meanwhile, even as the U-2 commenced its active career, efforts were under way to make it less vulnerable - The hope was to reduce the vehicle's radar cross-section, so that it would become less susceptible to detection. New developments in radar-absorbing materials were tried out and achieved considerable success, though not enough to solve the problem. Various far-out designs were explored, most of them seeking to create an aircraft capable of flying at extremely high altitudes, though still at relatively slow speed. None of them proved practicable.

Eventually, in the fall of 1957, Bissell arranged with a contractor for a job of operations analysis to determine how far the probability of shooting down an airplane varied respectively with the plane's speed, altitude, and radar cross-section. This analysis demonstrated that supersonic speed greatly reduced the chances of detection by radar. The probability of being shot down was not of course reduced to zero, but it was evident that the supersonic line of approach was worth serious consideration. Therefore, from this time on, attention focused increasingly on the possibility of building a vehicle which could fly at extremely high speeds as well as at great altitudes, and which would also incorporate the best that could be attained in radar-absorbing capabilities.

Lockheed Aircraft Corporation and Convair Division of General Dynamics were informed of the general requirement, and their designers set to work on the problem without as yet receiving any contract or funds from the government. From the fall of 1957 to late 1958, these designers constantly refined and adapted their respective schemes.

Bissell realized that development and production of such an aircraft would be exceedingly expensive, and that in the early stages at least it would be doubtful whether the project could succeed. To secure the necessary funds for such a program, high officials would have to receive the best and most authoritative presentation of whatever prospects might unfold. Accordingly, he got together a panel consisting of two distinguished authorities on aerodynamics and one physicist, with E. H. Land of the Polaroid Corporation as chairman. Between 1957 and 1959 this panel met about six times, usually in Land's office in Cambridge. Lockheed and Convair designers attended during parts of the sessions. So also did the Assistant Secretaries of the Air Force and Navy concerned with research and development, together with one or two of their technical advisors. One useful consequence of the participation of service representatives was that bureaucratic and jurisdictional feuds were reduced virtually to nil. Through the program both Air Force and Navy gave valuable assistance and cooperation.

As the months went by, the general outlines of what might be done took shape in the minds of those concerned. Late in November, 1958, the members of the panel held a crucial meeting. They agreed that it now appeared feasible to build an aircraft of such speed and altitude as to be very difficult to track by radar. They recommended that the President be asked to approve in principle a further prosecution of the project, and to make funds available for further studies and test. The President and his Scientific Advisor, Dr. James

Killian, were already aware of what was going on, and when CIA officials went to them with the recommendation of the panel, they received a favorable hearing. The President gave his approval.

Two Major Aerospace Firms Were Asked to Bid on a "Blackbird" Contract

Lockheed and Convair were then asked to submit definite proposals, funds were made available to them, and the project took on the code name "GUSTO".

Less than a year later the two proposals were essentially complete, and on 20 July 1959, the President was again briefed. This time he gave final approval, which signified that the program could get fully under way.

The next major step was to choose between the Lockheed and Convair designs. On 20 August 1959, specifications of the two proposals were submitted to a joint DOD/USAF/CIA selection panel:

	Lockheed	Convair
Speed	Mach 3.2	Mach 3.2
Range (total)	4,120 n.m.	4,000 n.m.
Range (altitude)	3,800 n.m.	3,400 n.m.
Cruise Altitudes		
Start	84,500 ft.	85,000 ft.
Mid-Range	91,000 ft.	88,000 ft.
End	97,600 ft.	94,000 ft.
Dimensions		
Length	102 ft.	79.5 ft.
Span	57 ft.	56.0 ft.
Gross Weight	110,000 lbs.	101,700 lbs.
Fuel Weight	64,600 lbs.	62,000 lbs.
First Flight	22 months	22 months

The Lockheed design was selected, Project "*GUSTO*" terminated, and the program to develop a new U-2 follow-on aircraft was named. On 3 September 1959, CIA authorized Lockheed to proceed with anti-radar studies, aerodynamic structural tests, and engineering designs, and on 30 January, 1960 gave the green light to produce 12 aircraft.

Pratt and Whitney Division of United Aircraft Corporation had been involved in discussions of the project and undertook to develop the propulsion system. Their J-58 engine, which was to be used in the A-12, had been sponsored originally by the US Navy for its own purposes, and was to be capable of a speed of Mach 3.0. Navy interest in the development was diminishing, however, and the Secretary of Defense had decided to withdraw from the program at the end of 1959. CIA's requirement was that the engine and airframe be further developed and optimized for a speed of Mach 3.2. The new contract called for initial assembly of three advanced experimental engines for durability and reliability testing, and provision of three engines for experimental flight-testing in early 1961.

The primary camera manufacturer was Perkin-Elmer. Because of the extreme complexity of the design, however, a decision was soon made that a back-up system might be necessary in the event the Perkin-Elmer design ran into production problems, and Eastman Kodak was also asked to build a camera. Minneapolis-Honeywell Corporation was selected to provide both the inertial navigation and automatic flight control system. The Firewell Corporation and the David Clark Corporation became the prime sources of pilot equipment and associated life support hardware.

Wind Tunnel Models of the "Blackbirds" Were Tested and Retested

The models were adjusted and readjusted, during thousands of hours in the wind tunnel.

Scale Model Wind Tunnel Test Performed by Lockheed Engineers

Kelly Johnson – Head of Lockheed "Skunk Works" [72] & [73]

Lockheed's chief designer was Clarence L. (Kelly) Johnson, creator of the U-2, and he called his new vehicle, not A-12 but A-11. Its design exhibited many innovations. Supersonic airplanes, however, involve a multitude of extremely difficult design problems. Their payload-range performance is highly sensitive to engine weight, structural weight, fuel consumption, and aerodynamic efficiency. Small mistakes in predicting these values can lead to large errors in performance.

Johnson was confident of his design, but no one could say positively whether the bird would fly, still less whether it would fulfill the extremely demanding requirements laid down for it. [68]

"Almost Everything Had to Be Invented"

This new aircraft was in a different category from anything that had come before. *"Everything had to be invented. Everything,"* [69] Johnson recalled. He committed *"Skunk Works"* to succeed in its toughest assignment to date: to have the innovative, challenging, envelope-bursting aircraft flying in a mere twenty months. [70]

Kelly Johnson – About to Fly a *"Blackbird"* Right Photo [72] & [73]
Chief Designer for P-38, P-80, F-104, U-2, A-12, YF-12A, M-21, D-21 Drone, SR-71, Etc

Kelly has received 44 aviation awards and was the first civilian VIP to complete the required training class and personally fly a *"Blackbird."* Kelly also has received forty-four U.S. patents. He has supervised over 40 plane designs or projects during his career at Lockheed, while also maintaining a ~ 2000 acre cattle ranch with ~300 cattle, purchased in 1963. He maintained his own equipment in a fully equipped 40 foot by 120 foot shop. During the time of the nuclear *"Cold War"* with the Soviets, Kelly designed the bridges on his ranch to support the weight of the Minuteman missiles, should they need to be relocated from nearby Vandenberg Air Force Base.

Kelly's Cattle Ranch Has Now Been Converted into a Vineyard [158]

Today's his ranch retained the same name *"Star Lane"* but was converted, after being sold in 1996, into a commercial vineyard, after his passing in 1990.[158]

69

Early Design Studies - Eleven Different Configurations Were Evaluated Before a Final Design Was Selected: (157)

Length: 116.67 Ft	Zero Fuel Weight: 41,000 Lbs	Cruise Mach: 3.0
Span: 49.6 Ft	Fuel Weight: 61,000 Lbs	Cruise Alt: 83 to 93 KFt
Height: 23.58 Ft	Takeoff Gross: 102,000 Lbs	Radius: 2,000 NM

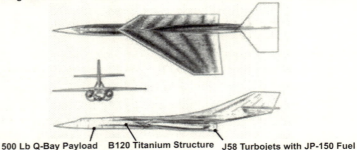

500 Lb Q-Bay Payload   B120 Titanium Structure   J58 Turbojets with JP-150 Fuel

Archangel 1 - July 1958

Archangel 1 Design Was Still Advanced

The A-1 (nicknamed Archangel - 1 by Lockheed) aircraft's empty weight was estimated at 41,000 pounds. With a capacity for 61,000 pounds of stored fuel, it would have had a gross weight of 102,000 pounds at takeoff. The A-1 was designed to cruise at a speed of Mach 3.0 and altitudes between 83,000 and 93,000 feet with a mission radius of 2,000 nautical miles. Later versions of the A-1 explored such options as canards mounted on the forward fuselage, a double-delta wing configuration, and winglets.

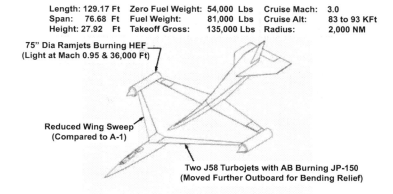

Length: 129.17 Ft	Zero Fuel Weight:	54,000 Lbs	Cruise Mach:	3.0
Span: 76.68 Ft	Fuel Weight:	81,000 Lbs	Cruise Alt:	83 to 93 KFt
Height: 27.92 Ft	Takeoff Gross:	135,000 Lbs	Radius:	2,000 NM

75" Dia Ramjets Burning HEF
(Light at Mach 0.95 & 36,000 Ft)

Reduced Wing Sweep
(Compared to A-1)

Two J58 Turbojets with AB Burning JP-150
(Moved Further Outboard for Bending Relief)

Archangel 2 - September 1958

Four engines were used for the A-2 which increased the dry plane weight by 13,000. pounds. The two extra engines were 75 inch diameter Ramjets which were started at Mach = .95

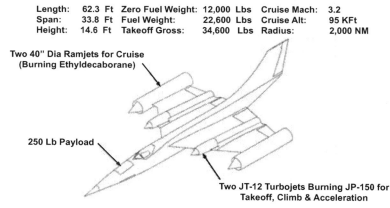

Length:	62.3 Ft	Zero Fuel Weight:	12,000 Lbs	Cruise Mach:	3.2
Span:	33.8 Ft	Fuel Weight:	22,600 Lbs	Cruise Alt:	95 KFt
Height:	14.6 Ft	Takeoff Gross:	34,600 Lbs	Radius:	2,000 NM

Two 40" Dia Ramjets for Cruise
(Burning Ethyldecaborane)

250 Lb Payload

Two JT-12 Turbojets Burning JP-150 for
Takeoff, Climb & Acceleration

Archangel 3 - November 1958

The A-3's two JT-12 powerplants were mounted at mid-span with the engine nacelle centered in the wing structure. These turbojets looked insignificant compared to the 40-inch-diameter ramjets on the wingtips. The turbojets would provide thrust for takeoff, climb, and acceleration while the ramjets would be used only during the cruise portion of the flight. The A-3 of November 1958 was Johnson's smallest design to date, just over 62 feet long with a wingspan of 33.8 feet. It had a gross takeoff weight of just 34,600 pounds and was expected to meet all performance requirements. A semi-tailless configuration (no horizontal stabilizer) reduced both weight and the radar cross section (RCS).

Johnson's A-4 was relatively small at 58 feet long with a 35-foot span. Its blended wing-fuselage configuration significantly reduced the RCS. The vertical stabilizer resembled a shark's dorsal fin running the length of the upper fuselage. A single J58 served as the main powerplant while two 34-inch-diameter ramjets on the wingtips provided cruise power. Maximum gross takeoff weight was estimated at 57,900 pounds.

In an attempt to further reduce size and weight, Johnson proposed the A-5. At a length of 46 feet and span of 32.5 feet, it came in at a gross weight of just 50,320 pounds but featured the most complex mix of powerplants yet. Two JT-12 turbojets buried in blended side fairings provided thrust for takeoff, climb, and landing. A centrally located 83-inch-diameter ramjet with a ventral intake provided cruise power while additional takeoff thrust came from a 10,000-pounds-thrust liquid-fueled rocket at the base of the vertical fin. In all other respects, the A-5 resembled a scaled-down A-4. Design integration was extremely challenging, particularly with respect to fuel accommodation.

Length:	64.0 Ft	Zero Fuel Weight:	29,200 Lbs	Cruise Mach:	3.2
Span:	47.2 Ft	Fuel Weight:	33,750 Lbs	Cruise Alt:	95 KFt
Height:	22.85 Ft	Takeoff Gross:	34,600 Lbs	Radius:	1,287 NM

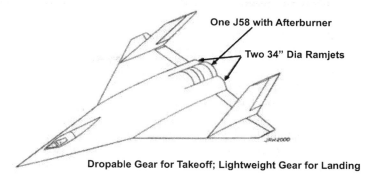

One J58 with Afterburner

Two 34" Dia Ramjets

Dropable Gear for Takeoff; Lightweight Gear for Landing

Archangel 6 - January 1959

For the A-6, Johnson proposed a configuration with a blended triangular forebody with delta wings with squared tips. Inwardly canted vertical fins were located about two-thirds of the way out from the wing roots. The powerplants included a single J58 and two 34-inch-diameter ramjets buried in the fuselage. With a length of 64 feet and a span of 47 feet, the airplane had a gross weight of 62,950 pounds. Weight penalties were reduced by equipping the airplane with lightweight landing gear. A detachable set of heavy-duty gear would be used for takeoff and drop away as soon as the craft lifted off the ground.

By January 1959, several things had become clear. Maximum performance and minimum RCS seemed to not occur simultaneously. The A-4 through A-6 designs lacked the necessary operational range. Skunk Works engineers noted that ramjet technology was not sufficiently mature for use in long-range cruise conditions. Two-stage systems, such as those involving a B-58 launch aircraft, were operationally impractical for multiple reasons including logistics and safety. Additionally, the customer was understandably anxious at this point to see a finished product. Johnson began to focus on a maximum-performance turbojet aircraft design with no performance concessions for the sake of improved RCS.

Johnson continued to refine the concept with the A-8 and A-9 designs but results were disappointing. Mission radius continued to hover around 1,637 nautical miles with a cruise altitude of slightly more than 91,000 feet, considerably less than the A-2 despite the weight reduction.

In February 1959 Johnson submitted the A-10 concept, an elegantly simple design. The 109-foot-long cylindrical fuselage featured a long forebody and was sharply tapered at each end. The semi-double-delta wings had squared tips and spanned 46 feet. A vertical tail fin with conventional rudder provided lateral stability. Two General Electric J93-3 turbojets would propel the airplane to speeds of Mach 3.2 at a 90,000-foot cruise altitude. At a takeoff weight of 86,000 pounds, the A-10 demonstrated a significant weight reduction (18,000 pounds) relative to the A-1 that allowed it to reach higher altitudes. Mission radius was estimated at 2,000 miles. RCS was still a problem, but Johnson was more concerned with performance.

Length:	116.67	Ft	Zero Fuel Weight:	36,800	Lbs	Cruise Mach:	3.2
Span:	56.67	Ft	Fuel Weight:	55,330	Lbs	Cruise Alt:	93.5 KFt
Height:	21.03	Ft	Takeoff Gross:	92,130	Lbs	Radius:	2,000 NM

Originally designed to carry 31,000 Lbs of HEF and 17,000 Lbs of JP-150

Key Operational Concept: Single Base + air refueling (13,340 NM Range with 2 air refueling/8 hour total mission time

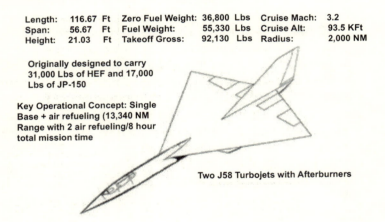

Two J58 Turbojets with Afterburners

Archangel 11 Design (March 1959) – Unacceptable RCS

The following month he refined the design further. The A-11 featured true double-delta wings spanning 56.67 feet. Fuselage length increased to 116.67 feet and the J93 engines were replaced with J58s. The A-11 was designed to take off from a home base, cruise at Mach 3.2 at 93,500 feet, and complete an eight-hour, 13,340-nautical-mile mission with two aerial refuelings.

Johnson pitched his A-11 concept to the CIA and reported the results of six months of radar studies. He emphasized that expected improvements to radar systems would enable detection of any airplane that might conceivably fly within the next three to five years. He specifically noted that the probability of detection of the A-11 was practically 100 percent. It was subsequently agreed the airplane might make such a strong radar target that it could be mistaken for a bomber. This was unacceptable for an airplane that was intended for use in clandestine reconnaissance missions. In July 1959, Johnson was surprised to learn that the CIA had offered to extend Lockheed's program and accept lower cruising altitudes in exchange for incorporation of RCS reduction techniques.

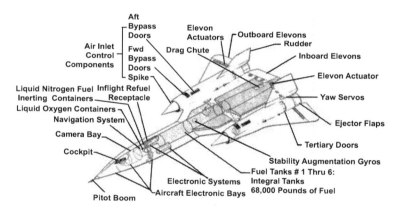

Archangel 12 Design Was Selected
(Initially Called A-11 by Lockheed's Kelly Johnson Before Later Renaming It to A-12)

The A-12 design incorporated features to maximize performance, survivability, and mission capability while minimizing weight, detectability, and (to the extent possible) cost. The fuselage contained no wasted space or extraneous material, and even the fuel did double duty as a coolant.

The airplane's fuselage consisted of a titanium structure of semi-monocoque construction with a circular cross-section. The sides flared out into sharply blended chines, assembled as interlocking saw-toothed wedges. On all A-12 airframes except those of the prototype and trainer variant, the outward-pointing teeth were fashioned from titanium while the interlocking, inward-pointing, teeth were made from radar-absorbent composites.

The sharply tapered nose section was pressurized and contained navigational and communications equipment, a remote compass transmitter, periscope optics, air inlet computer and angle transducer, and other radio equipment. A combination pitot-static and alpha-beta probe was installed at the forward tip to capture airspeed and altitude data.

The pilot's cockpit featured a V-shaped windscreen and was enclosed by an aft-hinged clamshell canopy. Both the windscreen and canopy featured windows with dual glass assemblies. The outer monolithic glass panels were separated from inner laminated glass panels by air gaps. An internal heated-air defrosting/defogging system, a deicing system, and an external rain-removal system insured good visibility in all weather conditions. The pilot's station was outfitted with conventional aircraft controls and instruments.

The crew cabin pressure could be set to 10,000 or 26,000-foot equivalent altitude pressurization. At altitudes below the pressure altitude selection, the cabin was essentially unpressurized. In theory, the pressurized cockpit allowed the pilot to operate in a standard flight suit with oxygen mask at altitudes below 50,000 feet but a full pressure suit was normally worn to ensure crew safety under normal as well as emergency conditions. In an emergency the pilot could jettison the canopy and egress using a rocket-propelled ejection seat at any altitude and Mach number within the flight envelope. A drogue chute stabilized the seat during descent until man-seat separation occurred automatically at a barometric altitude of 15,000 feet.

The electronic compartment (E-bay) was located just aft of the pilot's cockpit. This pressurized and air-conditioned space contained most of the communication and navigation equipment as well as the stability augmentation system, autopilot, flight reference, Mach trim, and other electronic systems.

The mission equipment bay (Q-bay) was located immediately aft of the E-bay and could be pressurized or unpressurized depending on specific equipment needs. This compartment provided space for installation of cameras and sensors, test packages, and/or ballast as dictated by mission requirements.

Air-conditioning equipment was located in the AC-bay, just aft of the Q-bay. This compartment housed most of the environmental control system equipment and the inertial navigation system. It also provided access to various circuit breakers and miscellaneous electrical components.

An in-flight refueling receptacle was located on top of the fuselage, just aft of the AC-bay. When de-energized, the receptacle doors formed the upper fuselage contour. When opened, the doors revealed a trough to accept the aerial tanker's refueling probe.

Another set of doors on the upper side of the aft fuselage provided a cover for the drag chute compartment. The drag chute, along with the wheel-braking system, aided airplane deceleration during normal landings or aborted takeoffs.

The underside of the fuselage featured nose and main landing gear wheel wells with hydraulically and mechanically actuated flush doors. The main gear wells also included insulated buckets to protect the tires from overheating while retracted during cruise.

Titanium Was Selected For The Primary Airframe Material

During the design phase, Lockheed evaluated many materials and finally chose an alloy of titanium to withstand these temperature and requirements. All the others, which would do so, were for the most part too heavy to be suitable for the purpose in hand. The forging for the landing gear would be the largest in the world out of titanium. [71]

To make the drawings and test the model was one thing; to build the aircraft was another. Many numerous problems arose from the simple fact that in flying through the atmosphere at its designed speed, the skin of the aircraft would be subjected to a temperature of more than 550 degrees Fahrenheit. For one thing, no metal yet commonly used in aircraft was suitable. Titanium, characterized by great strength, relatively lightweight, and good resistance to high temperatures was suitable, however, titanium was also scarce and very costly. Methods for milling it and controlling the quality of the product were not fully developed. Of the early deliveries from Titanium Metals Corporation, some 80 percent had to be rejected, and it was not until 1961, when a delegation from headquarters visited the officials of that company, informed them of the objectives and high priority of the Program, and gained their full cooperation, that the supply became consistently satisfactory. But this only solved one initial problem.

Titanium Was a Significant New Material That Hadn't Been Used for Major Airframe Parts Before

Some Growing Pains for the SR-71 Were Expected and Experienced:

One of the virtues of titanium was its exceeding hardness, but this very virtue gave rise to immense difficulties in machining and shaping the material. Drills, which worked well on aluminum, soon broke into pieces; new ones had to be devised.

When the Blackbird program first started, the drill bits for rivet holes in B-120 titanium could only drill ~17 holes, before having to be discarded. [151] By the end of the program, a newly shaped drill bit, developed in West Germany, allowed 100 holes and it could also be resharpened to drill another 100. Today's Titanium Nitride (TiN) coated bits (gold colored) will drill about 300 holes.

The engineers also discovered that spot welded wing panels fabricated during the summer had a low strength. Thankfully they documented their results, since those fabricated during the winter were much stronger. The water treatment facility in Burbank was adding chlorine to their water during the summer in order reduce algae. Since titanium reacts with chlorine, converting to distilled water, when cleaning parts, solved their problem.

It was also discovered cadmium plated wrenches were leaving trace amounts of cadmium on the bolts, which would cause galvanic corrosion when in contact with the titanium and cause the bolts heads to fall off. This happened after one or two exposures to temperatures over 600^0F. This discovery led to all cadmium tools to be removed from the workshop.

A new cutting fluid also had to be developed because the old one corroded titanium.

The best forge in the US could only produce 20% of the pressure needed to form these new titanium parts, thus new expensive forges were needed or incur the extra machining cost until the forges were fabricated. [151] Many titanium forgings were made oversized, and the parts machined to final shape, during the program.

Even the electrical wiring needed a new insulation to be developed, made of Kevlar and Asbestos. Early flights had

~17% failures with the electrical wiring measuring oil pressure and the flights had to be cut short.

Assembly-line production was impossible; each of the small fleet was, so to speak, turned out by hand. The cost of the program mounted well above original estimates, and it soon began to run behind schedule. One after another, however, the problems were solved, and their solution constituted the greatest single technological achievement of the entire enterprise. Henceforth it became practicable, if expensive, to build aircraft out of titanium.

Since every additional pound of weight was critical, adequate insulation was out of the question. The inside of the aircraft would be like a moderately hot oven. The pilot would have to wear a kind of space suit, with its own cooling apparatus, pressure control, oxygen supply, and other necessities for survival. The fuel tanks, which constituted by far the greater part of the aircraft, would heat up to about 350 degrees, so that a special fuel had to be supplied and the tanks themselves rendered inert with nitrogen. Lubricating oil was formulated for operation at 600 degrees F, and contained a diluent in order to remain fluid at operation below 40 degrees. Insulation on the plane's intricate wiring soon became brittle and useless. During its lifetime, the wiring and related connectors had to be given special attention and handling at great cost in labor and time.

Attaching Quartz Glass To The Metal Frame Was a Major Challenge

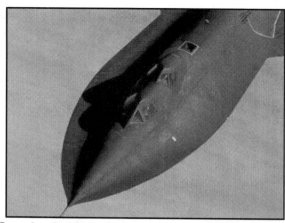

The Cockpit Windows are 2.0 Inches Thick "*Double Pane*" <u>Laminated Quartz</u> Glass. [74]

Something was Needed to Withstand the Abuse Without Distorting The Pilot's Vision

There was the unique problem of the camera window. The bay was to carry a delicate and highly sophisticated camera, which would look out through a quartz glass window. The effectiveness of the whole system depended upon achieving complete freedom from optical distortion despite the great heat to which the window would be subjected. Thus, the question was not simply one of providing equipment with resistance to high temperature, but of assuring that there should be no unevenness of temperature throughout the area of the window.

It took three years of time and two million dollars of money to arrive at a satisfactory solution. The program scored one of its most remarkable successes when the quartz glass was successfully fused to its metal frame by an unprecedented process. This involved the use of high frequency sound waves to attach quartz glass to the metal frame, such as the camera lens and the cockpit.

A Low Radar Cross Section Was Needed

Another major problem, of different nature, was to achieve the low radar cross-section desired. The airframe areas giving the greatest radar return were the vertical stabilizers, the engine inlet, and the forward side of the engine nacelles. Research in ferrites, high-temperature absorbing materials and high-temperature plastic structures was undertaken to find methods to reduce the return. Eventually the vertical tail section fins were constructed from a kind of laminated "*plastic*" material - the first time that such a material had been used for an important part of an aircraft's structure. With such changes in structural materials, the A-11 was renamed the A-12, and as such was never publicly disclosed.

To test the effectiveness of anti-radar devices, a small-scale model is inadequate; only a full-size mock-up will do. Lockheed accordingly built one of these, and as early as November 1959, transported it in a specially designed trailer truck over hundreds of miles of highway from the Burbank plant to the test area. Here it was hoisted to the top of a pylon and looked at from various angles by radar. Tests and adjustments went on for a year and a half before the results were deemed satisfactory. In the course of the process, it was found desirable to attach some sizable metallic constructions on each side of the fuselage, and Kelly Johnson worried a good deal about the effect of these protuberances on his design. In flight tests, however, it later developed that they imparted a useful aerodynamic lift to the vehicle, and years afterward, Lockheed's design for a supersonic transport embodied similar structures.

Pilots Needed to be Extraordinary - Only 93 Pilots Flew the "Blackbirds" and Only Three Made It To 1,000 Flight Hours.

Pilots for the program would obviously have to be of quite extraordinary competence, not only because of the unprecedented performance of the aircraft itself, but also because of the particular qualities needed in men who were to fly intelligence missions. Brigadier General Don Flickinger, of the Air Force, was designated to draw up the criteria for selection, with advice from Kelly Johnson and from CIA Headquarters. Pilots had to be qualified in the latest high performance fighters, emotionally stable, and well motivated. They were to be between 25 and 40 years of age, and the size of the A-12 cockpit prescribed that they be under six feet tall and under 175 pounds in weight.

Air Force files were screened for possible candidates and a list of pilots obtained. Psychological assessments, physical examinations and refinement of criteria eliminated a good many. Pre-evaluation processing resulted in sixteen potential nominees. This group underwent a further intensive security and medical scrutiny by the Agency. Those who remained were then approached to take employment with the Agency on a highly classified project involving a very advanced aircraft. In November 1961, commitments were obtained from five of the group. The small number recruited at this stage required that a second search be undertaken.

When the final screening was complete, the pilots selected for the program were William L. Skliar, Kenneth S. Collins, Walter Ray, Lon Walter, Mele Vojvodich Jr., Jack W. Weeks, Ronald "Jack" Layton, Dennis B. Sullivan, David P. Young, Francis J. Murray, and Russell Scott. After the selection, arrangements were made with the Air Force to effect appropriate transfers and assignments to cover their training and to lay the basis for their transition from military to civilian status. Compensation and insurance arrangements were similar to those for the U-2 pilots.

Construction of a Secret Base for Testing

One thing to be decided in the earliest stages of the program was where to base and test the aircraft. Lockheed clearly could not do the business at Burbank, where the aircraft was being built, if for no other reason that its runway was too short. The ideal location ought to be remote from metropolitan areas; well away from civil and military airways to preclude observation; easily accessible by air; blessed with good weather the year round; capable of accommodating large numbers of personnel; equipped with fuel storage facilities; fairly close to an Air Force installation; and possessing at least an 8,000 foot runway. There was no such place to be found.

"Area 51" is Selected Among the Final Candidates for Testing of "Blackbirds"

Ten Air Force bases programmed for closure were considered, but none provided the necessary security and realistic operating cost, as most of them were unacceptable. Edwards Air Force Base in California seemed a more likely candidate, but, in the end, it also was passed over.

Construction Begins in "Area 51"

Instead, a secluded site in Nevada was finally picked now nicknamed *"Area 51."* It was deficient in personnel accommodations and storage, and its long-unused runway was inadequate, but security was good, or could be made so, and a moderate construction program could provide sufficient facilities. Lockheed estimated what would be needed in such respects as monthly fuel consumption, hangars and shop space, housing for personnel, and runway specifications.

 Armed with the list of major requirements, Headquarters came up with a construction and engineering plan. And in case anyone became curious about what was going on at this remote spot, a cover story stated that the facilities were being prepared for certain radar studies, to be conducted by an engineering firm with support from the Air Force. The remote location was explained as necessary to reduce the effect of electronic interference from outside sources.

Excellent as it may have been from the point of view of security, the site at first afforded few of the necessities and none of the amenities of life. It was far from any metropolitan center. Lockheed provided a C-47 shuttle service to its plant at Burbank, and a chartered D-18 (Lodestar) furnished transportation to Las Vegas. Daily commuting was out of the question, however, and the construction workers arriving during 1960 were billeted in surplus trailers.

A New Runway is Constructed in Area 51

The A-12, YF-12, M-21 & SR-71 Were Developed and Flight Tested Here – Area 51 or Groom Lake [83] - Recent Satellite View of 8,500 Feet Long Paved Runway [75]

A new water well was dug, and a few recreational facilities provided, but it was some time before accommodations became agreeable.

Personnel Needed Housing While Working in Area - Trailers Were Moved to Area 51 [76]

Among the lesser snags, one existed because the laws of Nevada required the names of all contractor personnel staying in the state for more than 48 hours to be reported to state authorities. It was generally felt that to list all these names and identify the companies involved would be likely to give the whole show away. The Agency's General Counsel, however, discovered that Government employees were exempted from these requirements. Thenceforth all contractor personnel going to the site received appointments as Government consultants, and if questions were asked, the reply could be that no one but government employees were at the site.

Construction began in earnest in September 1960, and continued on a double-shift schedule until mid-1964. One of the most urgent tasks was to build the runway, which according to initial estimates of A-12 requirements, must be 8,500 feet long. The existing asphalt runway was 5,000 feet long and incapable of supporting the weight of the A-12. The new one was built between 7 September and 15 November and involved pouring over 25,000 cubic yards of concrete. Another major problem was to provide some 500,000 gallons of JP-7 aircraft fuel per month. Neither storage facilities nor means of transporting fuel existed. After considering airlift, pipeline, and truck transport, it was decided that the last-named was the most economical and could be made feasible by resurfacing no more than eighteen miles of highway leading into the base.

Three surplus Navy hangars were obtained, dismantled, and erected on the north side of the base. Over 100 surplus Navy housing buildings were transported to the base and made ready for occupancy. By early 1962 a fuel tank farm was ready, with a capacity of 1,320,000 gallons. Warehousing and shop space was begun and repairs made to older buildings. All this, together with the many other facilities that had to be provided, took a long time to complete. Meanwhile, however, the really essential facilities were ready in time for the forecast delivery date of Aircraft No. 1 in August 1961.

Delays With the New Engine Required An Alternate

The facilities were ready, but the aircraft was not. Originally promised for delivery at the end of May 1961, the date first slipped to August, largely because of Lockheed's difficulties in procuring and fabricating titanium. Moreover, Pratt & Whitney found unexpectedly great trouble in bringing the J-58 engine up to requirements. In March 1961, Kelly Johnson notified Headquarters:

"Schedules are in jeopardy on two fronts. One is the assembly of the wing and the other is in satisfactory development of the engine. Our evaluation shows that each of these programs is from three to four months behind the current schedule."

To this Bissell replied: *"I have learned of your expected additional delay in first flight from 30 August to 1 December 1961. This news is extremely shocking on top of our previous slippage from May to August understanding as of our meeting 19 December that the titanium extrusion problems were essentially overcome. I trust this is the last of such disappointments short of a severe earthquake in Burbank.* "

Realizing that delays were causing the cost of the program to soar, Headquarters decided to place a top-level aeronautical engineer in residence at Lockheed to monitor the program and submit progress reports.

Delays nevertheless persisted. On 11 September, Pratt & Whitney informed Lockheed of their continuing difficulties with the J-58 engine in terms of weight, delivery, and performance. Completion date for Aircraft No.1 by now had slipped to 22 December 1961, and the first flight to 27 February 1962. Even on this last date, the J-58 would not be ready, and it was therefore decided that a Pratt & Whitney J-75 engine, designed for the F-105 and flown in the U-2, should be used for early flights. The engine, along with other components, could be fitted to the A-12 airframe, and it could power the aircraft safely to altitudes up to 50,000 feet and at speeds up to Mach 1.6.

When this decision had been made, final preparations were begun for the testing phase. In late 1961 Colonel Robert J. Holbury, USAF, was named Commander of the base, with an Agency employee as his Deputy. Support aircraft began arriving in the spring of 1962. These included eight F-101's for training, two T-33's for proficiency flying, a C-130 for cargo transport, a U-3A for administrative purposes, a helicopter for search and rescue, and a Cessna-180 for liaison use. In addition, Lockheed provided an F-104 to act as chase aircraft during the A-12 flight test period.

Meanwhile in January 1962, an agreement was reached with the Federal Aviation Agency that expanded the restricted airspace in the vicinity of the test area. Certain FAA air traffic controllers were cleared for the Project; their function was to insure that aircraft did not violate the order. The North American Air Defense Command established procedures to prevent their radar stations from reporting the appearance of high-performance aircraft on their radar scopes.

Refueling concepts required prepositioning of vast quantities of fuel at certain points outside the United States. Special tank farms were programmed in California, Eielson Air Base-Alaska, Thule Air Base-Greenland, Kadena Air Base-Okinawa Island, Japan, and Adana, Turkey. Since the A-12 used a specially refined fuel, these tank farms were reserved exclusively for use by the Program. Very small detachments of technicians at these locations maintained the fuel storage facility and arranged for periodic quality control fuel tests.

At the Lockheed Burbank plant, Aircraft No. 1 (serial numbered 121) received its final tests and checkout during January and February 1962, and was partially disassembled for shipment to the site.

It became clear very early in planning that because of security problems and the inadequate runway, the A-12 could not fly from Burbank. Movement of the full-scale radar test model has been successfully accomplished in November 1959, as described above. A thorough survey of the route in June 1961, ascertained the hazards and problems of moving the actual aircraft, and showed that a package measuring 35 feet wide and 105 feet long could be transported without major difficulty. Obstructing road signs had to be removed, trees trimmed, and some roadsides leveled. Appropriate arrangements were made with police authorities and local officials to accomplish the safe transport of the aircraft. The entire fuselage, minus wings, was crated, covered, and loaded on the special-design trailer, which cost $100,000. On 26 February 1962, it departed Burbank, and arrived at the base according to plan.

Construction and Assembly Begins

Upon arrival, reassembly of the aircraft and installation of the J-75 engines began. Soon it was found that aircraft tank sealing compounds had failed to adhere to the metals, and when fuel was put into the tanks, numerous leaks occurred. It was necessary to strip the tanks of the faulty sealing compounds and reline them with new materials. Thus occurred one more unexpected and exasperating delay in the program.

Construction of a "*Blackbird*" at Lockheed's Plant in Burbank, California. [77]

Special Transportation of the Airframe Was Required

Special Design Trailer to Transport the Fuselage [78]

Finally, on 26 April 1962, Aircraft 121 was ready. On that day, in accordance with Kelly Johnson's custom, Louis Schalk took it for an unofficial, unannounced, maiden flight lasting some 40 minutes - As in all maiden flights, minor problems were detected, but it took only four more days to ready the aircraft for its first official flight.

On 30 April 1962, just less than one year later than originally planned, the A-12 officially lifted her wheels from the runway. Piloted again by Louis Schalk, it took off at 170 knots, with a gross weight of 72,000 pounds; and climbed to 30,000 feet. Top speed was 340 knots and the flight lasted 59 minutes. The pilot reported that the aircraft responded well and was extremely stable. Kelly Johnson declared it to be the smoothest official first flight of any aircraft he had designed or tested. The aircraft broke the sound barrier on its second official flight, 4 May 1962, reaching Mach 1.1. Again, only minor problems were reported.

With these flights accomplished, jubilation was the order of the day. The new Director of Central Intelligence, Mr. John McCone, sent a telegram of congratulation to Kelly Johnson. A critical phase had been triumphantly passed, but there remained the long, difficult, and sometimes discouraging process of working the aircraft up to full operational performance.

At "Blackbird" Altitudes and Temperatures, Oxygen Can Be Explosive

Oxygen can spontaneously ignite in the tanks and fuel lines at "*Blackbird*" altitudes. In order to reduce this chance, all of the fuel tanks are purged with pure nitrogen before being filled.

Purging the Fuel Tanks with Pure Nitrogen [79]

The "*Blackbird*" also carries 260 liters of liquid nitrogen in 3 canisters. This nitrogen expands into its gaseous form as it is pumped into the fuel tanks to top them off as fuel is consumed. Without the nitrogen, the empty fuel tanks would cavitate from the increased pressure when returning to lower altitudes to refuel. [29] The tanks are pressurized to 1.5 psi above ambient pressure.

Nitrogen is also used to pressurize the TEB ignition storage tank to provide operating supply pressure. TEB will ignite spontaneously when exposed to air at temperatures above -5C (23⁰F). The TEB storage tank is cooled by the main burner fuel flow. [80]

The last SR-71 flight was made on Saturday October 9, 1999; at the Edwards AFB air show. The aircraft used was NASA 844. The aircraft was also scheduled to make a flight the following day, but a fuel leak grounded the aircraft and prevented it from flying. The NASA SR-71s were then put in flyable storage, where they remained until 2002. They were then sent to museums. This aircraft made 734 flights during its service life, including 56 NASA flights. It accrued a total of 2,353.6 flight hours and was placed on display at the Dryden Flight Research Center at Edwards AFB. [81] During its career, no SR-71 was ever lost due to hostile actions. In fact, neither enemy fighters nor enemy surface to air missiles (SAM) were ever able to shoot down or to damage a SR-71, although one A-12 experienced minor damage, but returned safely. The SR-71 was the only production Air Force plane in history to retire formally without the loss of a single crew member.

But the aircraft was never shot down also because it was hardly detected by enemy radars, the *"Blackbird"* being the first aircraft to feature stealth technology. Its wings and fuselage were covered with a special iron ferrite coating, which absorbed radar energy instead of returning it to the sender. The SR-71 tail was made of a special composite material capable of 800^0 F, another first. The airplane shape was also designed to reduce the radar return signature. Its fuel was even stealthy.

With an RCS (Radar Cross Section) of a small light aircraft, when the SR-71 was found on radar it was too late for a SAM computer site to estimate its direction and for a missile to catch it for a successful kill.

Area 51 (Groom Lake) is a Highly Restricted
Location for Secret Testing – The Most
Protected Base on the Planet [84]

The SR-71 flight test were moved to Edwards Air Force Base after President Johnson made the public announcement of its existence.

An Underground Facility is Constructed For the "Blackbird"

Underground Test Facility in Area 51 for Plane Concealment from Foreign Satelitte Photography During Radar Testing

The range and the bearing of the SR-71 were also denied to the enemy by jamming its devices with the use of the sophisticated electronic countermeasures (ECM) transported by the "*Blackbird*". [82]

Radar Testing of a Full Size Aircraft Model in Area 51

Radar testing required hiding the plane from Russian satellites and photography during flyovers. The Plane is Mounted Upside Down on a Telescoping Pole, that was Retractable to Store the Plane Underground, When Soviet Satellites Passed Over [85]

Cold War Memorial at the Base of Mount Charleston [86]

A Fleet of "Blackbird" Spy Planes Was Ready

The *"OXCART"* Fleet in 1964 [87]

Operational Mission From Kadena Air Base on Okinawa Island, Japan

Most of The "*OXCARTS*" Operational Missions Were Flown Out Of Kadena Air Base On Okinawa, Japan [88]

Facing changed circumstances in relations with the Soviet Union and in US satellite development, US policymakers and intelligence officials had to come to grips with how best to use the A-12 as it neared completion. Its intended purpose, replacing the U-2 in overflights of the Soviet Union, had become less and less likely well before the A-12 was operational. Soviet air defenses had advanced to the point that even an aircraft flying faster than a rifle bullet at the edge of space could be tracked. In any event, President Kennedy had stated publicly that the United States would not resume such missions. The Director of Central Intelligence (DCI) McCone was determined to find a use for the aircraft—which he later described as "*quite invulnerable except under miraculous circumstances*" when it met design specifications. [89] But he lost the argument then, as well as later, when making the case for deploying the A-12 to help determine whether the Soviets had constructed an antiballistic missile system around Leningrad. By 1965, moreover, the photo reconnaissance satellite programs had progressed to the point that manned flights over the Soviet Union were unnecessary to collect strategic intelligence.

96

The Cuban missile crisis of October 1962 drew attention to the program because of the threat the U-2 faced from Cuban air defenses. U-2s regularly overflew the island after nuclear missiles were discovered there in mid-October, but two weeks after the discovery, a U-2 was shot down by a Cuban surface-to-air missile. Regular high-altitude reconnaissance of Cuba might no longer be possible. The A-12 now had a potential mission, and achieving operational status became a priority. Because of continued difficulties in achieving design requirements with the J58 engine, however, the A-12 would have to be flown only at up to Mach 2.8 at below 80,000 feet.

This risky program, codenamed "*SKYLARK*", was accelerated during the summer of 1964, after Soviet Premier Nikita Khrushchev declared that after the US elections in November, U-2s flying over Cuba would be shot down. In August, Acting DCI Marshall Carter ordered that "*SKYLARK*" be operationally ready by 5 November 1964 in case Khrushchev carried out his threat. [90] A detachment of five pilots and ground crew was organized to validate camera performance and qualify pilots for Mach 2.8 operations. They would have to go into action without the full complement of ECMs, as only one of the several devices planned would be available by the deadline, and Agency technical officers were certain that the Cubans would detect the flights and could shoot down the A-12s.

Khrushchev's Threat Was Bluster

The A-12 never was used against Cuba. US officials were still discussing the possibility nearly two years later, however, and CIA officials regarded Cuban overflights as a potentially productive way to test the A-12's ECMs in a hostile area, where weather was a factor. Agency analysts judged that the Soviets most likely would react to the flights privately and in low key. The 303 Committee—the NSC group that reviewed sensitive intelligence operations—rejected the idea because it "*would disturb the existing calm prevailing in that area of our foreign affairs.*" [91]

East Asia was the next area US leaders considered using the A-12. The People's Republic of China (PRC) had successfully tested a nuclear device in October 1964, and US military activity in Vietnam was increasing. Overhead collection would be the most important method for monitoring the Chinese program and the military situation in Vietnam, but satellites did not have a quick reaction capability, and several U-2s and drones had been lost over China. US military and intelligence officials drew up a plan for flying aircraft out of Kadena Air Base on Okinawa under a program called "*BLACK SHIELD*". The Pentagon made available nearly $4 million to provide support facilities on the island, which were to be ready by early fall 1965.

Meanwhile, North Vietnam was starting to deploy SAMs around Hanoi, and a concerned Secretary of Defense McNamara inquired in June 1965 about substituting A-12s for U-2s for reconnaissance over the North. CIA said that "*BLACK SHIELD*" missions could be flown over Vietnam as soon as operational performance requirements were achieved. With an overseas deployment looming, personnel at the A-12 test site went all out to have the aircraft meet mission requirements by late 1965. Improvements came faster than expected.

In August, DCI Raborn, who replaced McCone in April 1965, notified President Johnson that an A-12 had successfully simulated an operational mission with two refuelings and three cruise legs. On each leg the aircraft reached its design cruising speed of Mach 3.1 at altitudes between 80,000 and 90,000 feet. The flight covered a total distance of 7,480 miles in just under five and a half hours; forty percent of that time was spent at cruising speed. Only three minor malfunctions occurred; significantly, none involved the air inlets and electrical systems or were related to high heat. [92]

"The Bird Should Leave Its Nest"

Kelly Johnson's firm managerial hand had gotten back on track. Four A-12s were selected for "*BLACK SHIELD*", and final validation flights were conducted during the fall.

During them, the A-12s flew faster, higher, and longer than ever before. On 12 November 1965, the CIA's director of special activities in charge of the program wrote to the Agency's director of reconnaissance that he was *"very pleased to announce that, in my judgment, the A-12 aircraft, its technical intelligence sensors, and its operating detachment are operationally ready.... The detachment is manned, equipped, and highly trained.... The aircraft system is performing up to specifications with satisfying reliability and repeatability."* Because of *"some as yet unexplainable phenomena at cruise conditions,"* the A-12 could not fly as far as originally intended, but missions could be designed to take that deficiency into account. By 20 November, the validation flights were complete, and all the pilots were Mach 3 qualified. Two days later, Johnson told the Agency that *"the time has come when the bird should leave its nest."* [93]

Soon after, CIA's Board of National Estimates (BNE) issued an assessment of the potential political implications of *"BLACK SHIELD"*. The Agency's most senior analysts judged that the PRC would quickly track over-flights of its territory but would not start a diplomatic controversy about them unless it shot down an aircraft. Doing so would occasion a major political and propaganda campaign, but "We do not believe that missions, whether or not any aircraft came down inside China, would significantly affect Peiping's broader calculations governing its policy toward the war in Vietnam." North Vietnam, "already subjected to heavy US air attack and reconnaissance...would attach little extra significance to the operation." Lastly, through various sources, the Soviet Union would soon get a fairly complete picture of the scope of *"BLACK SHIELD,"* but *"would probably take no action and make no representations on the matter."* [94]

Analyses such as the BNE's informed the approval process for proposed missions. The steps were the same as for U-2 flights: an NSC-level recommendation and a Presidential authorization. After the A-12 passed its final tests, in early December the 303 Committee ordered the development and maintenance of a quick-reaction capability by January, 1st

99

1966, with deployment to Okinawa 21 days after the President issued his go order.

Then, nothing happened for more than a year. The 303 Committee approved none of CIA's five deployment requests, submitted with support in most instances from the Joint Chiefs of Staff and the PFIAB. Community analysts continued to believe the Chinese, North Vietnamese, or Soviets would not react publicly and belligerently to the missions. Siding with top State and Defense officials, however, the committee did not believe the intelligence requirements at the time - including warning of Chinese intervention in the Vietnam war—were so urgent as to justify the political risk of basing the detachment at Okinawa or revealing some of the A-12's capabilities to hostile nations.

In addition, some reluctance to use the A-12 was related to the discussion that had already begun about phasing out the CIA program. In mid-August 1966, President Johnson listened to the divergent views and upheld the 303 Committee's decision not to fly actual missions for the time being. [95]

Biding Time and Sharpening Procedures

During these months personnel worked on refining mission plans and flight tactics, testing the aircraft and systems, training, and preparing the forward base at Kadena. The delay was beneficial. Even though the A-12 had been declared operationally ready, important components in the propulsion system still needed correction. More efficient procedures reduced the time required to go from mission notification to deployment from 21 to 15 days. Six operationally configured aircraft were constantly training and engaging in operational flight simulations.

In October 1966, one week after its first flight, Article 127 flew for seven hours and 40 minutes, the longest time in air so far. Two months later, Lockheed test pilot Bill Park completed an impressive demonstration of the A-12's capabilities by flying 10,198 miles in six hours at an average speed of 1,659 mph (including slowdowns for refueling) - setting a speed and distance record unattainable by any other aircraft. By mid-February 1967, 2,299 test and training flights had been flown over 3,628 hours, with more than 332 of those at Mach 3 or higher.

First Fatality of the A-12 Program

The first fatality of the A-12 program occurred on 5 January 1967, when Article 125 crashed, killing CIA pilot Walter Ray. Because of a faulty fuel gauge and related electrical equipment problems, the aircraft ran out of fuel while on its descent to the test site. Ray ejected at between 30,000 and 35,000 feet but did not separate from the seat. That kept the parachutes from deploying, and he fell to earth, dying on impact.

To protect the security of the A-12 program, the Air Force informed the media that an SR-71 was missing and presumed down, and identified the pilot as a civilian. Like the three crashes that preceded it, Ray's involved a problem inherent in any new aircraft - a malfunction of a part specifically designed and built for it. None of the four incidents occurred while the A-12 was being subjected to the unprecedented rigors of design speeds and altitudes.

"OXCARTS" first operational mission over Southeast Asia was in May 1967. With pilot Mel Vojvodich in the cockpit, Article 131 refueled three times during its 3 hour 39 minute flight. By early 1967, the Johnson administration was growing anxious that the North Vietnamese could deploy surface-to-surface missiles (SSM) targeted at the South without being detected.

Missions Begin: Spying on the Enemy
Early Missions Over Southeast Asia

When the President asked for a collective proposal, CIA suggested that the A-12 be used, noting that its camera

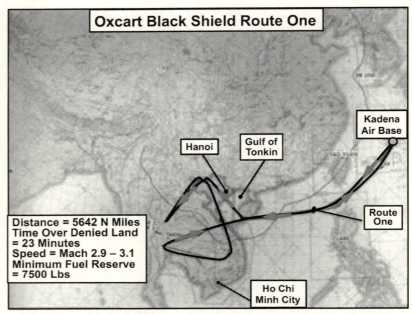

Oxcart Black Shield Route One

Kadena Air Base

Hanoi

Gulf of Tonkin

Route One

Distance = 5642 N Miles
Time Over Denied Land = 23 Minutes
Speed = Mach 2.9 – 3.1
Minimum Fuel Reserve = 7500 Lbs

Ho Chi Minh City

was better than those on drones or the U-2, and that it was much less vulnerable than those platforms and more versatile than the "*CORONA*" satellites.[97] elms brought up the idea at a luncheon with the President on 16 May and got his approval. The Agency put the "*BLACK SHIELD*" deployment plan into effect later that day.

"Blackbird" Route Over Vietnam

On 17 May, the airlift of personnel and equipment to Kadena began, and Articles 131, 127, and 129, flown by Vojvodich, Layton, and Weeks, arrived between 22 and 27 May. The first two flew non-stop from Nevada to Kadena; the third diverted at Wake Island to correct an equipment malfunction and finished the trip the next day. The unit, which at its inception had been designated for security purposes as the 1129th US Air Force Special Activities Squadron (SAS), Detachment 1, comprised three A-12s, six pilots (three deployed at a time; later two), and over 250 support personnel. Its commander was Col. Hugh "Slip" Slater, who had worked with CIA on the U-2 program and at the test site. The 1129th SAS was ready for operations by the 29th. The call came the next day to fly the first mission on the 31st over North Vietnam.

Image of the Hanoi Area [98]

This image of Hanoi area was taken during the fourth mission, on 30 June 1967.

The mission was a success, photographing 70 of the 190 known SAM sites and nine other priority targets, including an airfield, a military training area, an army barracks, and the port at Haiphong. No SAM facilities were located. Contrary to some published accounts, neither Chinese nor North Vietnamese radar tracked the aircraft nor did North Vietnam fire any missiles at it. Those hostile reactions did not occur until the third and 16th missions, respectively. [99]

Through 6 May 1968—the date of what would become the last flight—the A-12 pilots at Kadena flew 29 missions out of 58 they were put on alert to perform: 24 over North

Vietnam; two over Cambodia, Laos, and the DMZ; and three over North Korea. The flights were distributed among the pilots: Collins and Layton had six, Vojvodich and Weeks got five, Murray did four, and Sullivan was on three. The aircraft were flown at between Mach 3.1 and 3.2 and a bit above 80,000 feet. At that height, above the jet stream, air turbulence was minimal, and the curvature of the earth showed beneath the black, star-flecked sky.

The A-12s' aeronautical components and photographic systems proved very reliable. Twenty-seven of the sorties were judged successful, based on the quality of photography returned; two were deemed partially successful or unsuccessful due to cloud cover or a camera malfunction. One mission had to be cut short after one pass because of an engine problem. None of the 29 cancelled alerts were the result of mechanical concerns; bad weather caused all but three, which were due to operational decisions. The A-12s were so fast that they typically spent only about 12.5 minutes over North Vietnam on a single-pass mission and 21.5 minutes on a double-pass route.

Project headquarters in the Washington DC area planned and directed all the A-12 missions. Their preparation followed this procedure: Each day at 1600 local time a mission alert briefing took place. If the weather forecast—the key variable in deciding whether to go ahead or cancel the sorties—seemed favorable, Kadena was alerted and given a flight profile about 28 to 30 hours before takeoff. The primary and back-up aircraft and pilots were selected. The A-12s—painted black and bearing no markings other than red tail numbers that were changed every mission—got thorough inspections and servicing, all systems were checked, and the cameras were loaded into the bays. On the evening before the day of the flight, the pilots received a detailed briefing of the route. Twelve hours before takeoff (H minus 12), headquarters again reviewed the weather over the target. If it was still favorable, preflight procedures continued.

On the morning of the flight, the pilots got a final briefing. The aircraft's condition was reported, weather forecasts were reviewed, and changes in the mission profile and relevant intelligence was communicated. At H minus 2, headquarters issued a "go/no-go" decision. At this point the weather forecast also had to be good for the refueling areas. If the mission was still on, the primary pilot received a medical examination, suited up, and squeezed himself into the aircraft. If any malfunctions developed, the back-up would be ready to fly one hour later. This proved necessary only once. On the second mission on 10 June 1967, the primary A-12 lost a fillet panel during refueling and returned to base, and the back-up completed the mission. On most "BLACK SHIELD" flights, the A-12s were airborne about four hours. The shortest complete mission in Southeast Asia lasted just over 3.5 hours; the longest took nearly 5.5 hours. The aircraft took on fuel two or three times, depending on the planned route, on each operational flight: once, soon after takeoff south of Okinawa, and once over Thailand for each pass it would make over the target area before it returned to Kadena.

After the A-12s landed, the camera film was removed from the aircraft, boxed, and sent by courier plane to a processing facility. At first the film was developed at the Eastman Kodak plant in Rochester, New York. That trip took too long for US military commanders who wanted the intelligence more quickly. By late summer, processing was shifted to an Air Force center in Japan, and the photography could be available to the US military in Vietnam within 24 hours after a mission was completed.

Less than two months into "BLACK SHIELD" analysts had enough evidence to conclude that North Vietnam had never deployed SSMs. By the end of 1967, the A-12 had collected clear, interpretable photography of all of North Vietnam except for a small area along the border with the PRC. The "BLACK SHIELD" missions provided valuable imagery of SAM sites, airfields and naval bases, ports, roads, and railroads, industrial facilities, power plants, and supply depots. Military planners and photo interpreters used the information to develop air and air defense order of battle estimates, assess bomb damage, and develop flight routes and target sets for bombing runs, enabling US pilots to accomplish their missions more effectively and in greater safety. Analysis of photography of the DMZ gave insights into North Vietnamese infiltration and supply routes and North Vietnamese and Viet Cong troop deployments. [(100)]

Photos Were Valuable to the President

President Johnson's national security adviser, Walt Rostow, recounted that the A-12 missions (along with those of the SR-71) *"were invaluable to the President."* Without them, he *"would never have allowed any tactical air operations in the North because he was extremely sensitive…to the possibilities of a bomb accidentally hitting a Chinese or Russian ship while it was unloading in the harbor, and he also was determined to keep civilian damage and casualties to a minimum."* Johnson *"usually chose the targets personally and insisted on approving each and every raid into the North…. Before signing off on a mission he calculated in his own mind whether the anticipated losses were worth the anticipated gains."* The A-12 and SR-71 photographs *"were the decisive factors in helping him to make up his mind."* [(101)]

Under Fire Over Vietnam

North Vietnam fired SAMs at *"BLACK SHIELD"* A-12s three times but caused damage only once. The first attempted shoot down occurred on the 16th mission on 28 October 1967. Flown by Dennis Sullivan, the aircraft was on its second pass, approaching Hanoi from the west, when an SA-2 was launched at it. Photographs taken during the mission show missile smoke above the SAM site and the missile and its contrail, heading down and away from the aircraft. The A-12's ECMs worked well, and the SAM, which was fired too late, was never a threat. [(101)]

The second incident, two days later, on the 18th mission, was the closest an *"OXCART"* aircraft ever came to being shot down. Sullivan again was the pilot. On the first pass between Hanoi and Haiphong, radar tracking detected two

SAM sites preparing to launch, but neither did. On the second pass toward Hanoi and Haiphong from the west, at least six missiles were fired from sites around the capital. The A-12 was flying at Mach 3.1 at 84,000 feet. Looking out the rear-view periscope, Sullivan reported seeing six vapor trails go up to about 90,000 feet behind the aircraft, arc over, and begin converging on it. He saw four missiles— one as close as 100 to 200 yards away—and three detonations behind the A-12. Six missile contrails appeared on mission photography.

A post-flight inspection at <u>Kadena</u> found that a piece of metal, probably debris from an exploded missile, had penetrated the lower right wing and lodged near the fuel tank. A *"BLACK SHIELD"* officer at Kadena noted that the A-12 pilots were *"showing considerable anxiety about overflying this area before we get some answers."* Helms ordered that missions be temporarily suspended. None was flown until 8 December. It and the following one two days later photographed the Cambodia-Laos-South Vietnam triborder area and were not sent over the North. (103)

Sorties over North Vietnam resumed on 15 December and continued until 8 March 1968—the next-to-last *"BLACK SHIELD"* flight. The first two flights took different paths than the Hanoi-Haiphong route followed by the A-12s that were shot at in late October. Another SAM was fired on mission 23 on 4 January 1968; that aircraft took the same route as those that had been attacked.

The missile, fired on the second pass like the others, was captured on photography from launch to detonation, well over a mile from the aircraft. Two of the next three flights over North Vietnam came in from the south rather than the east, and all three stayed farther away from Hanoi and Haiphong than those that had been shot at. The general times when these flights were made did not change despite the SAM attacks; all crossed into North Vietnamese territory in the late morning.

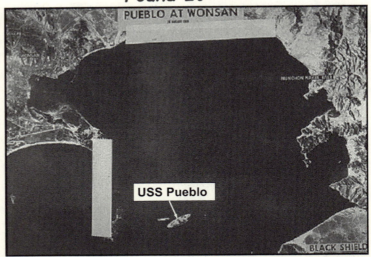

Missing Pueblo Ship Found at Wonsan

The North Korean seizure of the US Navy ship Pueblo, while it was on an intelligence mission, in international waters on 23 January 1968 enabled the A-12 to demonstrate its superiority as a quick-reaction collection platform. Although the US military had indicated its interest in *"BLACK SHIELD"* over-flights of North Korea even before the incident, the Department of State had opposed them, and none was planned when the Pueblo was captured. Walt Rostow remembered that *"[t]he whole country was up in arms over this incident. The President was considering using airpower to hit them [the North Koreans] hard and try to shake our crewmen loose. But when we cooled down, we had to suck in our gut and hold back until we were sure about the situation."*

Helms urged use of the A-12 to find the missing ship. Johnson was reluctant at first to offer such a *"tempting target"* but was assured that the aircraft *"could photograph the whole of North Korea, from the DMZ to the Yalu River, in less than 10 minutes, and probably do so unobserved by air defense radar. Which is precisely what happened."* [105]

On 24 January the Pueblo advisory group—comprising senior officials from the White House, the Departments of Defense and State, and CIA—had Helms draw up a reconnaissance plan that included A-12s. President Johnson approved their use later that day. [55] On the 26th, Jack Weeks flew a three-pass mission over the southern part of North Korea and the Demilitarized Zone. The purpose was to determine whether Pyongyang, which claimed it had caught the United States spying inside its territorial waters, was mobilizing for hostilities. Chinese radar tracked the A-12, but no missiles were fired during the highly successful mission.

Substantial intelligence was acquired on North Korea's armed forces; no signs of a military reaction were detected; and the Pueblo, apparently undamaged, was found in a small bay north of Wonsan accompanied by two patrol boats. [106] *"So we had to abandon any plans to hit them with airpower,"* according to Rostow. *"All that would accomplish would be to kill a lot of people, including our own."* But the A-12's photographs *"provided proof that our ship and our men were being held. The Koreans couldn't lie about that, and we immediately began negotiations to get them back."* [105] After difficult and protracted discussions, North Korea released the surviving crewmembers 11 months later.

The US military wanted a second over-flight of North Korea, but the Pueblo advisory group decided not to recommend any more right away because the *"excellent"* photography taken on the 26th, along with other information, was deemed sufficient to answer the crucial questions. By mid-February, however, the need returned. After the Department of State accepted assurances that it was highly unlikely the A-12 would come down in hostile territory, if something went wrong, the 303 Committee approved two more missions over the peninsula. They were flown on 19 February and 6 May. On the first sortie, scattered clouds concealed the area where the Pueblo had been spotted. (The ship had been moved by then.) The second flight - the last A-12 mission, as it turned out - was piloted by Jack Layton. Like the other missions over North Korea, it found no sign of a military buildup. [107]

Even after the Cold War ended with the Soviets, verifying with photographs, such as events during Chernobyl was important. Chernobyl was the worst nuclear accident in history, that required the evacuation of 49,000 people. A SR-71 provided verification. [108]

Sonic Booms at Low Altitudes
(Comments from Kelly Johnson) [109]

"Flight planning had to be done very carefully because of sonic boom problems. We received complaints from many sources. One such stated that his mules on a pack-train wanted to jump off a cliff when they were "boomed." Another complained that fishing stopped in Yellowstone Park, if a boom occurred, because the fish went down to the bottom for hours. I had my own complaint when one of my military friends 'boomed' my ranch and broke my $450 plate glass window. I got no sympathy on this, however."

Neither on this nor on other long flights was there serious trouble from sonic booms. To be sure, the inhabitants of a small village some 30 miles from the "*Area 51*" site were troubled as the aircraft broke through the sound barrier while gaining altitude. A change of the aircraft's course remedied this. With this change, the plane produced no more than an ominous rumble to the residents and since the plane was invisible to the naked eye of village residents, no one complained of this sound.

(Comment About Sonic Booms by the Author of This Book)

Many Americans have never heard a sonic boom, since supersonic flights now do not occur over populated areas of the United States. It is a very loud bang and recent CFD analysis and measurements indicate the pressure spike can be as high as ~45 PSI. Right around the time of the Cuban missile crisis (1962), a ~12 foot long crack developed in the ceiling of my parent's home, just as a very load boom was heard in the sky. The local newspaper later explained that the noise was from a super-sonic advanced government plane. Afterwards, as my dad was repairing the crack with a putty knife, I asked him why he didn't try to get the government to pay for it? He replied – *"Too much red tape and this was his contribution to help out in the "Cold War" with Russia."*

Comments from <u>Dr Bob Abernethy</u> About Pratt's J58 Engine
(Dr Bob is the Patent Holder of the J58 Engine Concept) [110]

"With a little knowledge of compressor aerodynamics, I could see at Mach 3 the front stages would be deep in stall from too low airflow and the rear stages were choked preventing the airflow to increase. The same problem exists when starting the engine and P&W solution was to open "start" bleeds. This brought the front stages out of stall and bypassed the rear stages. In October, 1958 the solution for all these J58 problems was clear to me. Bypass the bleed air around the compressor at high Mach number into the afterburner and it would solve the surge problem, provide cool air to afterburner and increase the mass flow and thrust significantly. Actually it converted the engine into a partial ramjet with capability above Mach 3! I called it the Recover Bleed Air engine on my patent. Here you see my drawing of the duct in my patent disclosure."

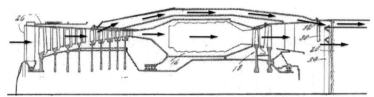

Schematic of Patent US 3,344,606 A (Granted in 1967 to Dr. Bob Abernethy)

Norm Cotter did not exactly leap for my solution, so I wrote him memo after memo for seven months trying to convince him. One of the problems was that if you open the bleed valves at high Mach number, there would be a hiccup in the airflow, which could unstart the inlet and possible destroy the aircraft. My solution was to open the valves at a lower Mach number, around 2.0 where there would be no bleed flow and no hiccup.

I finally convinced Norm on a Monday in April 1959. Norm immediately convinced Bill Brown, who called his buddy, Kelly Johnson, on a crypto phone and explained the concept of the Recover Bleed Air engine, emphasizing the Mach 3+ capability. Kelly flew to Washington and had **funding for the "Blackbird" by weeks end**. *The aircraft flew with J75s just about two years later from a top secret base, now known as Area 51 north of Las Vegas. We called it the "Sandpatch." About a year later they flew with the J58-D20 engines."*

Design Philosophy at that Time – "*Build Em and Break Em*" was the design philosophy, in that era, since accurate analytical analysis was not developed at that time in history. If a problem occurred, often five new solutions would be developed on paper, to solve the problem. For complex high priority problems, many times several of those designs would be built and tested until an acceptable solution was found. Pratt had its own complete machine shop, sheet metal, welding, coatings, materials, inspection, etc and could fabricate the vast majority of the engine parts very rapidly. Often, the designers could see and hold their newly designed parts within weeks instead of the months that it takes today. If a new solution was holding up an engine test, experimental parts would often be fabricated from a sketch without any design reviews or approvals – just fix the problem as fast as possible. The author of this book never knew of a single part that needed to be produced again from a drawing mistake. Engineers were held accountable, so they quickly checked their work two or three times. Also separate independent "*Checkers*" were available and always used. Questions and problems brought up by the machinist to the designer were answered verbally for experimental designs and the drawings would be changed later. Drawings were hand drawn and with no computer generated drawings. The exact configuration of each engine was kept on paper index cards and easily determined in minutes.

The *"Build Em and Break Em"* philosophy also applied to engine test. The engine would be run until something broke. The broken part would be beefed up and tested until something else broke.

Lockheed originally sketched the airframe configuration with five engineers using a spare door laid between two desks as a drafting table (per Ben Rich of Lockheed).

Origins of J58 Engine [111]

The J58 had its origins in a bigger JT-9 (J91) engine. The J58 was a 3/4 scale with a mass flow of 300 lb/sec, down from 400 lb/sec, and known by the company designation JT11. [112] The JT11 was initially proposed for the US Navy, hence its Navy designation J58. [112] It was also promoted for various Navy and Air Force aircraft, which never materialized, for example the Convair F-106, North American F-108, Convair B-58C, Vought XF8U-3 Crusader III, and North American A3J Vigilante. [112]

The J58 was initially developed for the US Navy [113] to power the planned version (using the J58) [114] of the Martin P6M jet flying boat. [115] The P6M started out using Allison J71-A-4 engines and then switched to the Pratt & Whitney J75 as the J58 wasn't ready due to development problems. Upon cancellation of this aircraft, it was selected between the Convair Kingfish and for the Lockheed A-12, YF-12A and SR-71. Sources link its origin to the USAF's requirement for a power plant for the WS-110A, the future XB-70 Valkyrie. [116]

113

The J-58 Engine Was Designed with Slide Rules Except For Occasional Help From a Computer for Rotating Disks

Slide Rules were used to design most of the J58 engine with very little computer analysis. Every design engineer had a slide rule at his or her desk and many had a small one in their shirt pocket. Thermal analysis was for one single steady state time point and most often the predicted temperature was a guess with very little calculations. At that time, calculators weighted 34 pounds and normally took over 15 minutes to determine a square root – most engineers left the calculator running, since it was very noisy, while they went to lunch, if accuracy was needed. Slide rule calculations were performed within three decimal point accuracy, if you had good eyesight. Finite element analysis was just starting to evolve and hand calculations took about one month of hard work with a slide rule to complete a spring rate analysis. Most of the designs tried to avoid any complex analysis or redundant structures – so *"KIS"* designs were employed – **K**eep **I**t **S**imple.

Most of the design and structural engineers had a copy of Roark's *"Formulas for Stress and Strain"* at their desk or had easy access to one. [117] If the exact formula was not available to analyze the design, a mathematician, Hank Barton, was available in the structures group to quickly derive the proper formula.

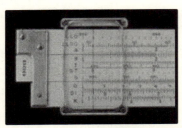

Slide Rule Used in the 1960's – Faster Than a 1960 Calculator [118]

Friden Calculator Used During Design of the J58 Engine [119] Weight = 34 Pounds

Occasionally an IBM 710 Computer Would be Used to Analyze One Time Point for a Rotating Disk [120]

Disk analysis was performed on a computer (an early IBM 710) however only one steady state analysis point was analyzed without any transient analysis, where the highest disk stresses occur. Safety factors were included to account for these transients.

A "Ferris Wheel" rig was used for cycling of blade loads and disk life verification. Stresses were measured with strain gauges to verify the calculations. [121]

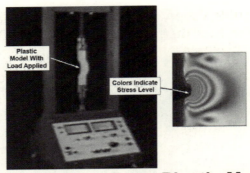

Plastic Model With Load Applied

Colors Indicate Stress Level

Photo-Elastic Test From Plastic Models to Determine Stress Concentration Factors [122]

Stress concentration factors were often determined by lab photo-elastic test of plastic models with a load applied, unless it could be found in *"Stress Concentration Design Factors"* by Peterson, first published in 1953. A few three dimensional stress models were performed if deemed necessary. Photo-elastic test have now been replaced with finite element modeling (FEM), since FEM is faster and produces about the same results.

Engine Revisions Required for Mach 3.2 Flight

The J58 for the A-12 had to be almost completely redesigned from its original Navy proposal (designed for Mach 3.0) so that it could operate continuously at Mach 3.2. The complete engine had to endure the temperatures of sustained flight at this speed and had to be designed accordingly.

The compressor redesign, as well as addressing the need for high temperature materials, such as Waspaloy in the compressor rear stages [123] had to address the aerodynamic shortcomings inherent in any turbo-machine compressor when ingesting very hot air (800 °F or 427 °C at Mach 3.2). [124] The route chosen to keep the J58 compressor pumping was to bleed air from the 4th stage compressor through 6 external ducts to the afterburner. In addition, a 2-position trailing edge flap was added to the inlet guide vanes. [125] This bleed and adjustable flap position kept the compressor working efficiently despite the high temperature air delivered to it by the intake.

The afterburner received the exhaust from the turbine as well as the bleed air from the compressor. Most of the compressor bleed was required for cooling the afterburner duct and propelling nozzle and the remainder was used, together with the turbine exhaust, to burn the afterburner fuel flow. [125]

The combustor liner and flame holders were sprayed with ceramic thermal barrier coating [72] to allow sustained afterburner operation at gas temperatures up to 3,200°F (1760 °C). [123]

J58 Engine Details

The engine is the Pratt and Whitney JT11D-20, designated "J58" by the military.

> The J58 engine is a single-spool, afterburning turbo-jet, with a 4th-stage variable flow area controlled by actuation, bleeding bypass duct air into the afterburner.
> The bleed system is operated at high Mach numbers to provide increased compressor stall margin – bleed air re-enters the engine ahead of the afterburner where the air is used for cooling and increased thrust augmentation.
> Bypass airflow is 20% of total flow into engine.
> Engine RPM is maintained by modulating the exhaust nozzle.
> This arrangement provides nearly constant airflow at a given Mach number from below military power to maximum afterburner, which is very desirable when operating behind a supersonic mixed compression inlet.

Fuel consumption at a cruising speed is approximately 8,000 gallons per hour.

117

Fuel is JP-7, which has a high flash point (140^0 F) and a high boiling point - 540 to 550^0F.

Combustors were 8 cans exiting into an annular duct fabricated of Hastelloy X. Each can had six fuel nozzles or a total of 48, for the engine.

To light JP-7 fuel a special ignition system was used. A chemical – pyrophoric triethylborane (TEB), ignites the main engine and the afterburner. It burns at a very high temperature. It was chosen as an ignition method for reliability reasons, and in the case of the *"Blackbird,"* because the JP-7 fuel is difficult to ignite.

Turbine is a two stage and the compressor is nine stages, both axial flow.

Air entering the combustor reaches 1400°F.

Turbine inlet temperature is ~2000°F.

Gas temperatures in afterburner section reaches 3200°F.

Ground starting used a AG330 cart, which required using two 325 HP Buick wildcat engines (some were 400 Hp) connected to a single J58 starter drive, spun at 3,200 RPM in order to fire the gas turbine engines up. An air turbine was later developed, which had less noise, since the Buicks did not have mufflers. The cockpit had a *"TEB Remaining Counter"* to keep track of the TEB (16 shots), but there was a platinum catalytic ignition system in the afterburner to back up the TEB system.

650 Horsepower Was Required to Start Each Engine

J58 Start Cart with Two Buick Wildcat "*Nailhead*" V8 Engines - 401 Cubic Inch, 325 Horsepower Each; Coupled Together. Located at the Seattle Museum of Flight

A few SR-71 were started with big block Chevy V-8 engines, since they were more available than the Buicks. An air turbine was developed later to start the SR-71, which had less noise.

General Characteristics of the J58 Engine [126]

Type: afterburning turbojet with compressor bleed bypass

Length: 17 ft 10 in (5.44 m) (an additional 6 in (15 cm) at max. temp.)

Diameter: 4 ft 9 in (1.45 m)

Dry weight: approx. 6,000 lb (2,700 kg)

Compressor: 9-stage, axial flow, single spool

Combustors: 8 can, annular

Turbine: two-stage axial flow

Fuel type: JP-7 from a special tanker or in an emergency JP-4 or JP-5 could be used from any tanker (limited to Max Mach 1.5) [127]

Maximum thrust: 32,500 Pounds with Afterburner; 20,500 Pounds without Afterburner

Overall pressure ratio: 7.5 at take off [128]

Specific Fuel Consumption = $\underline{\text{1.9 Lbm/Hr}}$ [129]
Lbs

Thrust-to-weight ratio: approx. 6.0

Air flow: 300 lb/sec (136 kg/s) at take off [128]

JP-7 Fuel used as hydraulic fluid – one of the first for airplanes [32]

The J58 Engine is Unique

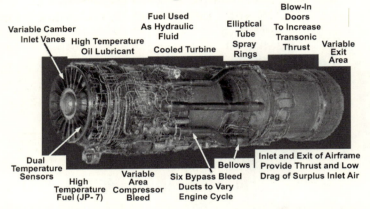

Variable Camber Inlet Vanes — High Temperature Oil Lubricant — Fuel Used As Hydraulic Fluid — Cooled Turbine — Elliptical Tube Spray Rings — Blow-In Doors To Increase Transonic Thrust — Variable Exit Area

Dual Temperature Sensors — High Temperature Fuel (JP-7) — Variable Area Compressor Bleed — Six Bypass Bleed Ducts to Vary Engine Cycle — Bellows — Inlet and Exit of Airframe Provide Thrust and Low Drag of Surplus Inlet Air

The Bellows Allow for Thermal Expansion Between Bypass Ducts and Engine Case [130]

A very unique feature of the J58 engine is the six bypass ducts that flow 4th stage compressor air into the turbine exhaust case and afterburner. Various experiments, with different flow areas, were conducted to vary the mass flow in order to arrive at ~20% flow.

Materials [131] - The development of the J58 brought with it some of the most challenging metallurgical development problems experienced by Pratt & Whitney Aircraft up to that time with components operating at unprecedented

120

levels of temperature, stress and durability. The J58 was a first for Pratt to cool its first turbine blade in production.

Premature cracking of the turbine airfoils, made from what was then conventionally-cast (i.e. equiaxed) Mar-M200, the strongest of the cast nickel-base alloys, was avoided with the development of directionally solidified parts cast in the same material. Directionally solidified Mar-M200 became the strongest cast turbine material in existence at that time and was introduced into J58 production engines. Single crystal turbine blades cast in Mar-M200, provided further improvements in high temperature properties would also be developed through testing in J58 engines.

Astroloy, the strongest known nickel-base superalloy in the Western world at that time, was also used for many of the rotating disks.

Inlet Guide Vanes – The inlet guide vanes of the J58 was another unique feature for that period in time. The vanes were variable in order to optimize airflow and reduce the risk of unstarts.

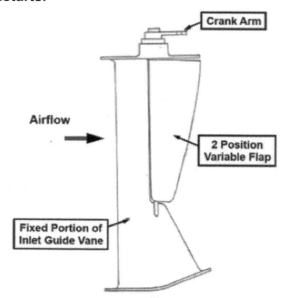

Variable Flow Area Inlet Guide Vanes

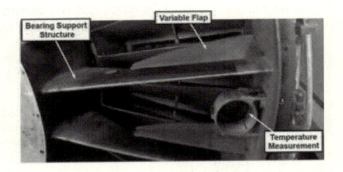

Front View of Variable Inlet Guide Vanes

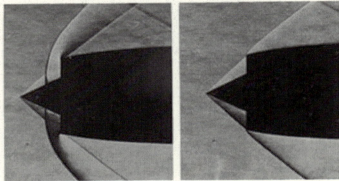

Unstarted Inlet   **Started Inlet**
Schlieren Flow Visualization

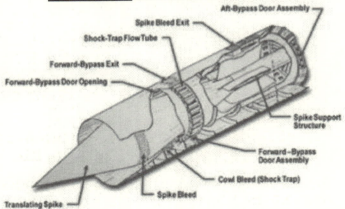

View of Inlet Spike and Bypass Door [132]

The Inlet design was led by <u>Ben Rich</u> of Lockheed, who later inherited Kelly Johnson's job as chief of their "*Skunk Works*".

Variable Inlet for the SR71 Engine

J58 Inlet With Spike Removed

J58 Inlet Spike – Translates Axially 26 Inches

Schematic of Inlet Spike

Forward Bypass Doors (Modulated)

Shock Bleed Trap

Centerbody Strut

Spike

Spike Actuator & Servo

Fwd Bypass

Centerbody Strut

Aft Bypass

Aft Bypass Servo

Spike Bleed (Slotted Surface)

Press Ratio Valve

Press Ratio Sensor

Pitot Tube

Spike and Bypass Doors Are Hydraulically Actuated

Spike Bleed Exit

Fwd Bypass Servo

Gear Door Switch

Inlet Spike is Translated Automatically with Manual Pilot Override (132)

Bypass airflow is ~20% of the total flow into the engine. At Mach 3.0, the inlet produces 54% of the overall thrust. The engine core accounts for 17% and the ejector 29% of the thrust. Each inlet is canted inward and downward to optimize airflow.

The spike translates a total of 26 inches to properly control the shock wave. A hydraulic actuator, computer controlled, provides operating forces up to 31,000 pounds. The outside ambient inlet temperature at 80,000 feet is minus 65 ^{0} F. The spike is locked in the forward position up to 30,000 feet. Above Mach 1.6, the spike retracts ~1.625 inches per .1 Mach number increase.

Pilot Lou Schalk said on his first *"unstart"* that he considered punching out because the ride was so rough, but he thought twice about it because things might not be better outside.

The Pratt J58 manager, Bill Brown, later suggested to Kelly Johnson that they install *"Mice"* in the inlet. Kelly followed through on this idea and the *"unstarts"* were reduced.

Close-up View of <u>Inlet</u> Installed with *"Mice"*
(133)

The engines were located about half way out on the wing span, so a great concern existed with the very high yawing moment that would develop should the inlet stall. Lockheed therefore installed accelerometers in the fuselage that immediately sensed the yaw rate and commanded the rudder booster to apply 9 degrees of correction within a time period of .15 seconds. This device

124

worked so well that the test pilots very often couldn't tell whether the right or left engine blew out. They knew they had a blowout, of course, by the buffeting that occurred with a *"popped shock."* Later an automatic restart device was developed, which keeps the engine out time to a very short period. [134]

J58 Inlet and Engine Operation Diagram [135]

The propulsion system consisted of the intake, engine, nacelle or secondary airflow and ejector nozzle (propelling nozzle). The propulsive thrust distribution between these components changed with flight speed: [136]

Mach 2.2   Inlet = 13%; Engine = 73%;   Ejector = 14%

Mach 3.2   Inlet = 54%; Engine = 17.6%; Ejector = 28.4%

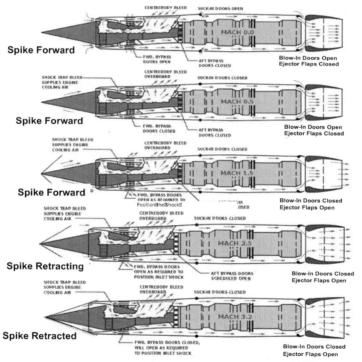

Variable Inlet Operation Diagram [137]

A Youtube video explaining the above operation is:
https://www.youtube.com/watch?v=F3ao5SCedlk

125

Right Photo Shows Shock Diamonds and Translucent Glowing Afterburner Case [138]
(At full afterburner, the case glows yellow and red).

Blow-In Doors

Nozzle and Ejector Flaps Cooling Air Entrance – "*Blow –In Doors*" With No Actuators - Moved by Air Pressure

Thermal Barrier Coatings Were New in The 1960's

© 2005, Robert Nocera

View of Five Zone Sprayrings Including Augmentor Liner [139]

J58 Engine Design Features, Some Development "Growing Pains" and a Few Stories or "Tales"

Turbine Blade Design – The first stage turbine blade was cooled with compressor air with a very simple one-pass cooling concept (a first for Pratt). At that time in history, it was thought that adding cooling holes into the airfoil wall would create a stress concentration of three, which would result in a very short life. It was not discovered until later into the next program that the stress concentration was much lower.

A water and steam cooled first stage turbine blade was designed and engine tested at a much higher turbine inlet temperatures and thrust. Since no missile ever came close to a kill for the SR-71, this design was never incorporated, since it was more complex and required an extra airframe water tank, although increased thrust was provided.

Airfoil creep of both 1st and 2nd blades, permanent growth or stretch of the airfoil, was the turbine blade limiting life factor. Since a large variation in material properties existed, each blade length was measured at engine overhaul and those deemed to not make it to the next overhaul were discarded.

Combustors – Since the combustor walls were very hot and required cooling with compressor air, an idea to evaluate an uncooled high temperature ceramic material arose, in order to relocate the cooling air to the fuel injector system. Ceramic combustor parts were built, however fractured into very small pieces during the first start of an experimental engine test.

The diffuser case was a telescoping design that allowed the combustor cans to be removed without the disassembly of the bearing compartments.

127

Thermal Growth & Cracks – Some cracks occurred in the engine static parts due to large differences in thermal growth, however the crack growth was normally slow to propagate in engine materials. Most engines materials were very ductile such as Waspaloy, Hastelloy X, Stainless steel and 6-4 Titanium. A standard solution was to replace the cracks with engineered "*keyhole slots*" and analyze the resultant leakage to determine if the slots were acceptable. Lockheed added corrugations to the airframe skin, so that when parts were heated during flight, drag would not increase with buckles.

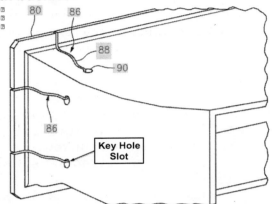

Keyhole Slots to Reduce Thermal Cracks [140]

Foreign Object Damage (FOD) - Various bolts, nuts, wrenches, and even a flashlight were ingested into the engine and caused damage, mainly to the first stage compressor blade. [141] The engine name-plate was even sucked into an engine and its mounting needed to be solved differently. A special program was initiated with signs, etc to remind personnel to be more careful. Engines were even hoisted into the air, at Lockheed, and shook, listening for any loose parts. Mechanics became very sensitive, since it was expensive, ~$250,000 for the flashlight incident, to repair the engine.

128

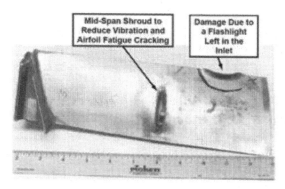

First Stage Titanium Compressor Blade After Hitting Inspector's Flashlight - Total Damage ~$250,000.

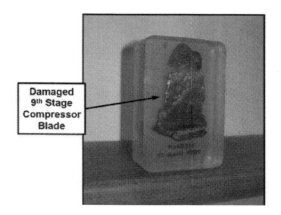

Rear Compressor Blade Damaged During Accident and Crash of a "*Blackbird*" Aircraft

Front View of the J58 Engine and a View of Mid-Span Shrouds on the First Stage Compressor Blades [142]

One day Kelly Johnson of Lockheed called the head of design at Pratt and Whitney, Ben Savin, and said they found a small dowel pin below the engine bay and the flight had been postponed waiting on his *"Go Ahead."* He wanted to know if the pin was important and it did not have a part number – just the size. The author of this book missed lunch that day looking for where the pin was used only to find out later, when Kelly called back, to tell us that they found where the pin was used – not in the engine.

Augmentor Liner Buckling [143] – At that time in history, the analytical structural method for sizing augmentor liners was elastic buckling, which is still used today for cold parts. However, the J58 discovered that a new phenomena, which Pratt called *"creep buckling"* existed. Creep buckling is after running the engine for some time at extreme temperatures; the material would soften and the part would collapse or buckle. More than five augmentor liners buckled into a small size and were shot out the exhaust into the pond behind the engine. The liners would be retrieved by boat, with a fishing device, to be evaluated until a method was developed to predict the collapse.

Augmentor Screech – A very loud noise would be emitted from the engine augmentor area under certain conditions. This noise could easily be heard from 20 miles away and nearby parts were quickly destroyed. Various design iterations of screech liners were experimentally evaluated until a satisfactory solution was found.

Fuel [144] - A new fuel was developed for the engine due to the harsh high operating temperatures and was produced by Shell Oil. JP-7 jet fuel was developed, by the USAF, for use in its supersonic aircrafts. It has a high flash point, and with a boiling point of around 550°F. It is thermally stable enough to be used in aircraft, that get incredibly hot from travelling at Mach 3+. Shell added an agent (PWA-536) in a concentration of at least 200 parts per million to make the fuel slippery and lessen the wear on the fuel pump, as it was also used as a hydraulic fluid. The latest Boeing X-51 "*Waverider*" also uses JP-7 fuel.

Because of these features, JP-7 is hard to ignite at normal temperatures, so a chemical "*starting fluid*" that ignited spontaneously with oxygen called triethylborane (TEB) [145] was injected into the engine to start it and also to ignite the afterburner in flight. The J-58 carries about 1.25 pints of TEB in a special pressurized tank on top of each engine, which is sufficient for at least 16 starts, restarts, or afterburner lights. This number was one of the limiting factors of SR-71 endurance, as after each air refueling, the afterburners had to be reignited. The TEB plumbing was made of special extra thick stainless steel wall tubes to reduce the effect of erosion, due to the chemical reaction. The TEB tanks were also cooled with fuel.

In 1958, Shell Oil vice president Jimmy Doolittle [146] arranged for the company developing the JP-7 fuel to manufacture several hundred thousand gallons of the new fuel. This fuel required the product Shell commonly used to make Flit insect repellant, causing a nationwide shortage of the product that year.

Coking in the internal engine fuel lines and fuel nozzles was common during shutdown, so separate heatshields, around the internal fuel tubes and fuel nozzles, were used to reduce the amount of coking. Fuel was dumped at shutdown by automatic valves, including a valve in the diffuser case wall to reduce the chance of coking of any excess fuel.

Fluid Leaks and Plumbing – A concern existed that plumbing joints (B-nuts) would occasionally leak and start a fire at the extreme temperatures. It was too hot for rubber O-rings, at that time, therefore all of the initial plumbing was brazed together at assembly to reduce the chance of any leak. Brazing was used for the initial engines, until a reliable metal soft deformable seal could later be developed. A special *"Voi-Shan"* soft metal seal was developed that proved to be reliable and reduced the time and expense to disassemble the engine. Lockwire was added for locking redundancy.

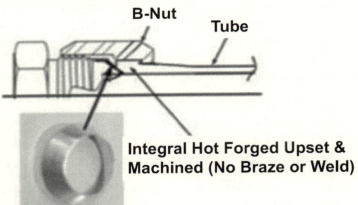

B-Nut

Tube

Integral Hot Forged Upset & Machined (No Braze or Weld)

37⁰ Conical Seal
(Soft Material)

A *"Soft Nickel Conical Seal"* was Developed to Eliminate Possible Leaks [147]

Disassemble and Reassembly of the Initial J58 Plumbing was a Pain without Coupling Nuts.

High cycle fatigue cracks of the plumbing braze joints was also a concern, therefore numerous configurations were tested on a *"Shaker Table"* to determine the configuration which had the highest fatigue life and later incorporated into the engines.

Gearbox Mount Problems and Drive Shaft

Twisting – As flight test increased to higher Mach numbers, new problems arose. One, which today may be considered simple with our modern computer techniques, concerned the remote gearbox. The gearbox mounts started to exhibit heavy wear and cracks, and the long driveshaft between the engine and the gearbox started to show twisting and heavy spline wear. After much slide-rule analysis, it was decided that the location of the gearbox relative to the engine was unknown at high Mach number transients. A test was devised to install a stylus on the engine and a scratch pad on the gearbox. It was measured that the gearbox moved ~4 inches relative to the engine. This was much more than the shaft and gearbox system

133

could take. Universal joints at both ends were added to solve the problem.

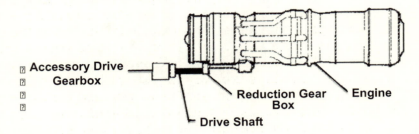

⬚ **Accessory Drive**
⬚   **Gearbox**
⬚
⬚

Reduction Gear Box   **Engine**

Drive Shaft

Relative Movement Between Engine and Accessory Drive Gearbox was Measured to be 4.0 Inches

Oil (PWA 524) - The J-58 required special <u>silicone-based oil</u> that didn't degrade at the extreme high temperatures. The oil was not free flowing at cold temperatures, as it was similar to molasses, so it was diluted with trichlorethylene, especially in cold weather. If a diluent was not used and the ambient temperature was low, starting the engine was *"Like a Rock."* Some initial tests were conducted by preheating the oil before starting.

Diffuser Case Material – One of the challenges of high Mach number flight is the resulting high temperature and the material selection of the diffuser case. Most of today's engines specify Inconel 718, however its capability was not suitable for speeds at Mach 3.2 and the long duration flights. <u>Waspaloy</u> was chosen for the J58 engine, however the casting technology for large complex structures in Waspaloy was not feasible at that time. The J58 diffuser case was a welding of various individual parts, however a special welding process for Waspaloy needed to be developed. This process required a number of iterations, and many engineers today think that Waspaloy can't be welded successfully.

Engine Mount Problem – A mounting-related problem occurred under certain conditions of down-load on the wing. At these conditions, the outer half of the nacelle would rotate into the engine and crush the engine plumbing and anything else in the way. Originally, the engine was mounted on a stiff rail structure at the top of the nacelle with a stabilizing link from the top of the engine rear mount ring to the aircraft structure as shown below. To solve the crushing problem, Pratt and Whitney Aircraft redesigned the rear mount ring so that a tangential link could be installed between the engine and the outboard side of the nacelle. This maintained a finite distance between the nacelle and the engine under all conditions.

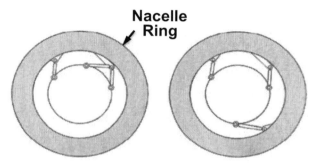

Nacelle Ring

Original Engine Mount on the Left; Modified Engine Mount on the Right

Control Cables – The engine had two mechanical fuel controls - one for the main combustor and another for the afterburner. Cables riding on pulleys connected these controls, and the pilot had only one throttle. As the engine heated up and grew thermally, the cable connecting the two mechanical fuel controls slowly changed lengths and would annoy the pilot by resetting the throttle position during flight. A special cable material was later specified - used for the mainspring in Elgin watches called "*Elgiloy*" and also a long cantilevered spring, which replaced the initial system and solved the annoying problem.

Augmentor Spray Ring – A variable flow area elliptical tube spray ring was used to reduce the maximum fuel pump pressures. The fuel flow was varied circumferential to reduce local hot spots, therefore experimental testing was used to optimize the fuel flow and augmentor liner metal temperatures.

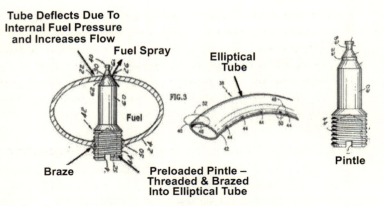

Tube Deflects Due To Internal Fuel Pressure and Increases Flow

Fuel Spray

Elliptical Tube

Fuel

FIG.3

Braze

Preloaded Pintle – Threaded & Brazed Into Elliptical Tube

Pintle

Patent # 4841725 Assigned to Excello Corp.

Cross Section of the Augmentor Spray Rings [148]

The afterburner is fully modulating with five spray rings zones

Gold Coated Plumbing - Gold plated external tubes were initially used to reduce the internal fluid temperatures. This gold coating was later removed to reduce cost and prevent theft of the gold. A gold nickel braze was still used due to its excellent ductility.

Reverse Flow from Turbine - Hot gas from the turbine/afterburner area would occasionally reverse flow at certain conditions, into the six bypass tubes and create higher temperatures in the compressor. Waspaloy material was used for the compressor blades, aft of the bypass tube entrance, to prevent over temperature.

Compressor Vane Cracking – Occasionally the compressor vanes would develop high cycle fatigue cracks due to dwelling too long while passing thru the vane natural frequency. The vanes were shot peened while waiting for a new redesign, which added damping and moved the natural frequency. Since the vanes never

136

cracked again after shot peening, the redesign was never incorporated.

Fastener Anti-Seize – Since engine operating temperatures were higher than those experienced before, many bolts would break during disassembly. Numerous coatings on the threads were evaluated to reduce the diffusion bonding and disassembly breakaway torque. A special modified thread and a coating compound was specified, which greatly reduced the problem.

Sniff Test – The engine front bearing compartment would occasionally leak a small amount of oil during shutdown. This was acceptable for the engine but not for the aircraft's pilot environmental system and pilot, since it had a foul smell. Various test were being conducted at Pratt for changes to eliminate this leak, however it was slow to determine if the changes were acceptable. The final and fastest test method to determine if the smell had been eliminated was to collect some engine air from a bleed port in a sanitary napkin and bottle. It was then sent to the project-engineering group and the assistant project engineer performed a "*smell test*." The test was not performed in front of the secretary.

Bet Between Lockheed and Pratt - Shortly after the start of development commenced, a wager was opened between Kelly Johnson and Bill Brown (head of J58 engine development at Pratt). The wager was over which of the two companies would succeed in producing the best fuel-injection system for the aircraft. It was settled that the loser would have to carry the cost for the use of the wind tunnel, which Brown estimated at $12,000. Pratt & Whitney won and true to promise, Kelly sent a check of sufficient value. The event was used to play a prank. Bill Brown acquired a complete naval sailor's uniform, with cap and blue jacket and had himself photographed in front of the 41.0 feet long private yacht of Bill Gordon (plant manager of Pratt). He sent the photograph to Kelly with the comment "*Thanks for the Check.*" The photograph hung for many years afterwards on the wall of Lockheed's staff reunion room. (149)

137

Full-Scale Fuel System Test Rig at Various Angles of Climb and Decent on Fuel Feed Capability

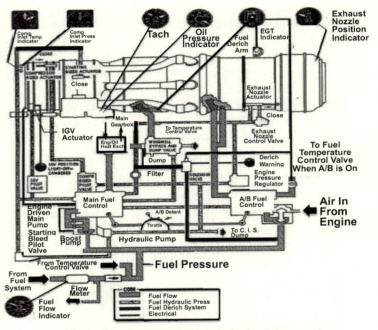

J58 Fuel System Schematic

In 1980, an improved digital fuel control was developed and replaced the analog fuel control. After the change, "*Unstarts*" became less frequent but not completely eliminated.

Test Engineer Award – In that era, it became a custom that the test engineer in charge of running the J58 engine would receive an award if the engine blew, while on their watch - no matter the reason. The award was an Indian statue and needed to be kept on their desk in plain sight until the next J58 blew, and then it was passed to the next test engineer. Norm Jones, now retired, was the last recipient of this award and still has it mounted in his home, 28 years after the SR-71 program was terminated.

Tale About His Dad's Ashes

Story about Pratt's J58 Manager – Bill Brown was a strong leader of the J58 group. One story was related to a trip with Norm Cotter to make a presentation at the Pentagon. In those days, if your charts included secret material, you had to be handcuffed to this long metal tube, coming and going, with the secret drawings inside. In those days, secret drawings were printed on pink paper to distinguish them from unclassified drawings. As a perk, you could fly first class if the trip was long and Bill hid the handcuffs in his suit cuff. The stewardess always wanted to check the tube into baggage, and of course, you couldn't. When Bill and Norm sat down in National Airline's plane, the stewardess said, *"Mr. Brown we will have to check that tube in baggage"*. Brown looked at her and said, *"I am sorry but you can't do that."* She said *"why not?"* He said because *"it's my father's ashes."* She was embarrassed and left, only to return shortly. She asked, *"if that's your father's ashes Mr. Brown, why is it so big?"* And Bill, deadpanned, said, *"He didn't all burn!"* The stewardess was shocked and Norm cracked up trying not to laugh.

Bill *"Catfish"* Brown and Dr Bob Abernethy – Pratt Employees

The J58 Engine Caught the Everglades on Fire More Than Once

Fires in the Everglades – More than once, a fire was started due to a surprise mishap of a J58 engine part being exhausted over a large pond and catching the Everglades on fire. A fire department and fire truck had been located on Pratt & Whitney property to handle these events. As the fire truck passed the main engineering building, with siren blasting, most of the J58 employees wondered who would work overtime that night solving the problem they helped created. It was a pain the first night of overtime, since many carpooled and needed a ride home late at night – most lived about 20 to 25 miles from the plant in the Everglades.

Some Believed That the J58 Engine Didn't Make a Lot of Noise

(Per Bob Abernathy)

A two star general happened to be at Edwards Air Force Base when an SR-71 landed and took off. He said, " Weren't those engines quiet!" Lockheed and P&W went into the panic mode to find out if the J58 engines were really quiet. Our P&W noise expert from East Hartford flew out to Edwards to assist Lockheed to run a special noise test on the SR-71. The data showed the SR71 was at least 6 dB lower than it should be...four times as quiet! Gordon Titcomb ordered me to find out why and fix the JTF17 (Pratt's SST engine) so it would be quiet. I assigned my best engineer, Ted Langston, and he produced a beautiful hypothesis that explained it all. The theory was that the J58 blow-in door ejector produced Aoelian tones caused by vortexes in the exhaust that shielded the noise. An Aeolian tone is the sound produced when subsonic flow passes over a long thin object like the wind in the forest blowing through pine needles. The word comes from the Greek mythology, the God of the wind, Aeolius. Ted developed a correlation of nozzles with and without blow-in door ejectors and started a test program to prove the hypothesis. He also made a sexy water table movie showing the vortexes in color."

Water Table Test and Movie of Flow Around the SR-71

"Gordon Titcomb called me in his office and said put together a "dog and pony show" and go convince the FAA, Boeing, and Lockheed that we know how to make the

141

JTF17 (supersonic transport) so quiet! I said no sir, we have not turned it on and turned it off. We have not proved the concept! Gordon said we can't wait. The competition is almost over. Do you want GE to win? So I pitched it to General Maxwell who ran the FAA program. He said, "Fantastic!" I went to Boeing and they loved it. At Lockheed, Dr. Stroud actually hugged me and said, "Bob. I believe it, I believe it!!!" Within a couple weeks we heard that GE added a blow-in door ejectors to their design. Then Boeing & GE won the competition and it was all over for us. About two months later the Russians put a blow-in door ejector on the TU144. Then our P&W East Hartford Noise Expert revisited Lockheed and found an error in their data reduction! As you all know, the J11 D-20 engine is **really loud!** When they cycle the afterburner at night in Florida, we can hear it on the coast about 20 miles away!"

Interested In Visiting a Museum and Seeing a "Blackbird"

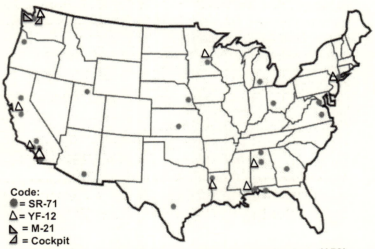

Code:
● = SR-71
△ = YF-12
◤ = M-21
◿ = Cockpit

Museums With a SR-71 or M-21 [153]

List of SR-71 Blackbird Locations [153]

#	AF Serial #	Model	Museum Location or Fate
1	61-7950	SR-71A	Lost, 10 January 1967
2	61-7951	SR-71A	Pima Air & Space Museum (adjacent to Davis-Monthan Air Force Base), Tucson, Arizona. Loaned to NASA as "YF-12A 60-6934".
3	61-7952	SR-71A	Lost, 25 January 1966
4	61-7953	SR-71A	Lost, 18 December 1969
5	61-7954	SR-71A	Lost, 11 April 1969
6	61-7955	SR-71A	Air Force Flight Test Center Museum, Edwards Air Force Base, California
7	61-7956	SR-71B	Air Zoo, Kalamazoo, Michigan
8	61-7957	SR-71B	Lost, 11 January 1968
9	61-7958	SR-71A	Museum of Aviation, Robins Air Force Base, Warner Robins, Georgia
10	61-7959	SR-71A	Air Force Armament Museum, Eglin Air Force Base, Florida
11	61-7960	SR-71A	Castle Air Museum at the former Castle Air Force Base, Atwater, California
12	61-7961	SR-71A	Kansas Cosmosphere and Space Center, Hutchinson, Kansas
13	61-7962	SR-71A	American Air Museum in Britain, Imperial War Museum Duxford, Cambridgeshire, England
14	61-7963	SR-71A	Beale Air Force Base, Marysville, California
15	61-7964	SR-71A	Strategic Air Command & Aerospace Museum, Ashland, Nebraska
16	61-7965	SR-71A	Lost, 25 October 1967
17	61-7966	SR-71A	Lost, 13 April 1967
18	61-7967	SR-71A	Barksdale Air Force Base, Bossier City, Louisiana
19	61-7968	SR-71A	Science Museum of Virginia, Richmond, Virginia
20	61-7969	SR-71A	Lost, 10 May 1970
21	61-7970	SR-71A	Lost, 17 June 1970
22	61-7971	SR-71A	Evergreen Aviation Museum, McMinnville, Oregon
23	61-7972	SR-71A	Smithsonian Institution Steven F. Udvar-Hazy Center, Washington Dulles International Airport, Chantilly, Virginia
24	61-7973	SR-71A	Blackbird Airpark, Air Force Plant 42, Palmdale, California
25	61-7974	SR-71A	Lost, 21 April 1989
26	61-7975	SR-71A	March Field Air Museum, March Air Reserve Base (former March AFB), Riverside, California
27	61-7976	SR-71A	National Museum of the United States Air Force, Wright-Patterson Air Force Base, near Dayton, Ohio
28	61-7977	SR-71A	Lost, 10 October 1968. Cockpit section survived and located at the Seattle Museum of Flight.
29	61-7978	SR-71A	Lost, 20 July 1972
30	61-7979	SR-71A	Lackland Air Force Base, San Antonio, Texas
31	61-7980	SR-71A	Dryden Flight Research Center, Edwards Air Force Base, California
32	61-7981	SR-71C	Hill Aerospace Museum, Hill Air Force Base, Ogden, Utah (formerly YF-12A 60-6934)

Locations of All of the SR-71's : Code = ☐ = Lost in Accident *(29 "A" Models; Two "B" Models; One "C" Model)*

Twelve Were Lost in Accidents - None Were Shot Down

#	AF Serial #	Museum Location or Fate
1	06924/#121	On display at the Blackbird Airpark in Palmdale, CA.
2	06925/#122	On display at the USS Intrepid Sea-Air-Space Museum in the New York City Harbor.
3	06926/#123	Lost on May 24, 1963 near Wendover, UT.
4	06927/#124	On display at the California Science Center in Los Angeles, CA.
5	06928/#125	Lost on January 5, 1967 at Groom Lake, NV.
6	06929/#126	Lost on December 28, 1967 at Groom Lake, NV.
7	06930/#127	On display at the U.S. Space & Rocket Center, Huntsville, AL.
8	06931/#128	On display at the Minnesota Air National Guard Museum, MN.
9	06932/#129	Lost on June 5, 1968 in the South China Sea off of the Philippines Islands.
10	06933/#130	On display at the San Diego Aerospace Museum, in San Diego, CA.
11	06934 - 06936	Numbers that were assigned to the YF-12A.
12	06937/#131	On display at the Southern Museum of Flight, Birmingham, AL.
13	06938/#132	On display at the USS Alabama Battleship Memorial Park, Mobile, AL.
14	06939/#133	Lost on July 9, 1964 at Groom Lake, NV.
15	06940/#134M	M-21: On display at the Museum of Flight, Seattle, WA.
16	06941/#135M	M-21: Lost on July 30, 1966 near Midway Island.

Locations of a YF-12 or a M-21

Five YF-12s Were Lost and One M-21 Was Lost

Code =   ☐   = Lost in Accident

A Development Cost Opinion About the "Skunk Works" Process By the Author of This Book

Development Cost Opinion – Design and development was in a different era when going to work was fun, with a new challenge arising almost daily. The feeling of **loyalty** was upward, downward and sideways, including especially the government. The work was pioneering, most never having been performed in the past, and it was very exciting.

The government understood clearly that the faster a successful design and development program was completed; the program cost would be minimized and reduced. Therefore, almost all *"micro-management"* and minute tracking of cost and status charts was non-existent. Almost all engineers worked on solving technical challenges with most approvals from just their supervisor. Honest strong program leaders were held accountable and felt empowered to get the job done and only reported on very high-level objectives. Their reputation and honor was at stake if they didn't succeed as promised. Therefore, I believe the program development cost is at least half of today's major military programs, which also have less innovation needed. Numerous *"Bean-Counting"* and *"Business Majors"* extend the program length, in my opinion, with cost status updates, including approvals, which drive up the cost instead of reducing it compared to a *"Skunk Works"* type process. This is just a minority opinion about a *"Skunk Works"* process.

Kelly Johnson's Fourteen "Skunk Works" Rules (154)

1) The *"Skunk Works"* manager must be delegated practically complete control of his program in all aspects. He should report to a division President or higher.

2) Strong but small project offices must be provided both by the military and industry.

3) The number of people having any connection with the project must be restricted in an almost vicious manner. Use a small number of good people (10% to 25% compared to the so-called normal systems).

4) A very simple drawing and drawing release system with great flexibility for making changes must be provided.

5) There must be a minimum number of reports required, but important work must be recorded thoroughly.

6) There must be a monthly cost review covering not only what has been spent and committed but also projected costs to the conclusion of the program.

7) The contractor must be delegated and must assume more than normal responsibility to get good vendor bids for subcontract on the project. Commercial bid procedures are very often better than military ones.

8) The inspection system as currently used by the Skunk Works, which has been approved by both the Air Force and Navy, meets the intent of existing military requirements, and should be used on new projects. Push more basic inspection responsibility back to subcontractors and vendors. Don't duplicate so much inspection.

9) The contractor must be delegated the authority to test his final product in flight. He can and must test it in the initial stages. If he doesn't, he rapidly loses his competency to design other vehicles.

10) The specifications applying to the hardware must be agreed to well in advance of contracting. The Skunk Works practice of having a specification section stating clearly which important military specification items will not knowingly be complied with and reasons therefore is highly recommended.

11) Funding a program must be timely so that the contractor doesn't have to keep running to the bank to support government projects.

12) There must be mutual trust between the military project organization and the contractor, the very close cooperation and liaison on a day-to-day basis. This cuts down misunderstanding and correspondence to an absolute minimum.

13) Access by outsiders to the project and its personnel must be strictly controlled by appropriate security measures.

14) Because only a few people will be used in engineering and most other areas, ways must be provided to reward good performance by pay not based on the number of personnel supervised.

Ending of Program

During November 1965, the very month the program was finally declared operational, the moves toward its demise commenced. Within the Bureau of the Budget, a memorandum was circulated expressing concern at the costs of the A-12 and SR-71 programs, both past and projected. It questioned the requirement for the total number of aircraft represented in the combined fleets, and doubted the necessity for a separate CIA fleet. Several alternatives were proposed to achieve a substantial reduction in the forecasted spending, but the recommended course was to phase out the A-12 program by September 1966 and stop any further procurement of SR-71 aircraft. Copies of this memorandum were sent to the Department of Defense and the CIA with the suggestion that those agencies explore the alternatives set out in the paper. But the Secretary of Defense declined to consider the proposal, presumably because the SR-7I would not be operational by September 1966.

Things remained in this state until in July 1966 the Bureau of the Budget proposed that a study group be established to investigate the possibility of reducing expenses on the SR-71 program. The group was requested to consider the following alternatives:

1. Retention of separate A-12 and SR-71 fleets, i.e., status quo.
2. Collocation of the two fleets.
3. Transfer of the mission and aircraft to SAC.
4. Transfer of the mission to SAC and storage of A-12 aircraft.
5. Transfer of the mission to SAC and disposal of A-12 aircraft.

The study group included C. W. Fischer, Bureau of the Budget; Herbert Bennington, Department of Defense; and John Parangosky, Central Intelligence Agency.

This group conducted its study through the fall of 1966, and identified three principal alternatives of its own. They were:

1. To maintain the status quo and continue both fleets at current approved levels.
2. To mothball all A-12 aircraft, but maintain the capability by sharing SR-71 aircraft between SAC and CIA.
3. To terminate the fleet in January 1968 (assuming an operational readiness date of September 1967 for the SR-71) and assign all missions to the SR-71 fleet.

On 12 December 1966 there was a meeting at the Bureau of the Budget attended by Mr. Helms, Mr. Schultze, Mr. Vance, and Dr. Hornig, Scientific Advisor to the President. Those present voted on the alternatives proposed in the Fischer-Bennington-Parangosky report. Messrs. Vance, Schultze, and Hornig chose to terminate the fleet, and Mr. Helms stood out for eventual sharing of the SR-71 fleet between CIA and SAC. The Bureau of the Budget immediately prepared a letter to the President setting forth the course of action recommended by the majority. Mr. Helms, having dissented from the majority, requested his Deputy Director for Science and Technology to prepare a letter to the

President stating CIA's reasons for remaining in the reconnaissance business.

On 16 December Mr. Schultze handed Mr. Helms a draft memorandum to the President which requested a decision either to share the SR-71 fleet between CIA and SAC, or to terminate the CIA capability entirely. This time Mr. Helms replied that new information of considerable significance had been brought to his attention concerning SR-71 performance. He requested another meeting after January 1st to review pertinent facts, and also asked that the memorandum to the President be withheld pending that meeting's outcome. Specifically, he cited indications that the SR-71 program was having serious technical problems and that there was real doubt that it would achieve an operational capability by the time suggested for termination of the A-12 program. Mr. Helms therefore changed his position from sharing the SR-71 aircraft with SAC to a firm recommendation to retain the A-12 fleet under civilian sponsorship. The Budget Bureau's memorandum was nevertheless transmitted to the President, who on 28 December 1966 accepted the recommendations of Messrs. Vance, Hornig, and Schultze, and directed the termination of the program by 1 January 1968.

This decision meant that a schedule had to be developed for orderly phase-out. After consultation with Project Headquarters, the Deputy Secretary of Defense was advised on 10 January 1967 that four A4 2's would be placed in storage in July 1967, two more by December, and the last four by the end of January 1968. In May Mr. Vance directed that the SR-71 assume contingency responsibility to conduct Cuban overflights as of 1 July 1967 and take over the dual capability over Southeast Asia and Cuba by 1 December 1967. This provided for some overlap between withdrawal and SR-71 assumption of responsibility.

Meanwhile, until 1 July 1967, the detachment was to maintain its capability to conduct operational missions both from a prepared location overseas and from the US. This included a 15 day quick reaction capability for deployment to the Far East and a seven-day quick reaction for deployment over Cuba. Between 1 July and 31 December 1967 the fleet would remain able to conduct operational missions either from a prepared overseas base or from home base, but not from both simultaneously. A quick reaction capability for either Cuban overflights or deployment to the Far East would also be maintained.

All these transactions and arrangements occurred before they had conducted a single operational mission or even deployed to Kadena for such a mission. As recounted above, the aircraft first performed its appointed role over North Vietnam on the last day of May 1967. In succeeding months, it demonstrated both its exceptional technical capabilities and the competence with which its operations were managed. As word began to get around that was to be phased out, high officials commenced to feel some disquiet. Concern was shown by Walt Rostow, the President's Special Assistant; by key Congressional figures, members of the President's Foreign Intelligence Advisory Board, and the President's Scientific Advisory Committee. The phase-out lagged, and the question was reopened.

A new study of the feasibility and cost of continuing the program was completed in the spring of 1968 and four new alternatives were proposed:

1. Transfer all aircraft to SAC by 31 October 1968; substitute Air Force for contractor support where possible; turn the test A-12 aircraft over to the SR-71 test facility.
2. Transfer as in alternative 1, above, and store eight SR-71's.
3. Close the home base and collocate the fleet with SR-71's at Beale Air Force Base in California, but with CIA retaining control and management.
4. Continue operations at its own base under CIA control and management.

Mr. Helms expressed his reactions to these alternatives in a memorandum to Messrs. Nitze, Hornig, and Flax, dated 18 April 1968. In it he questioned why, if eight SR-71's could be stored in one option, they could not be stored in all the options, with the resultant savings applied in each case. He questioned the lower cost figures of combining the with the SR-71's and disagreed, for security reasons, with collocating the two fleets. Above all, however, he felt that the key point was the desirability of retaining a covert reconnaissance capability under civilian management. It was his judgment that such a requirement existed, and he recommended that continue at its own base under CIA management.

In spite of all these belated efforts, the Secretary of Defense on 16 May 1968 reaffirmed the original decision to terminate the program and store the aircraft. At his weekly luncheon with his principal advisers on 21 May 1968, the President confirmed Secretary Clifford's decision.

Early in March 1968, USAF SR-71 aircraft began to arrive at Kadena to take over the *"BLACK SHIELD"* commitment, and by gradual stages the A-12 was placed on standby to back up the SR-71. The last operational mission flown by was on 8 May 1968 over North Korea, following which the Kadena Detachment was advised to prepare to go home. Project Headquarters selected 8 June 1968 as the earliest possible date to begin redeployment, and in the meantime flights of A-12 aircraft were to be limited to those essential for maintaining flying safety and pilot proficiency. After *"BLACK SHIELD"* aircraft arrived in the US they would proceed to storage. Those already at base were placed in storage by 7 June.

During its final days overseas, the enterprise suffered yet another blow, as inexplicable as it was tragic. On 4 June Aircraft No. 129, piloted by Jack Weeks, set out from Kadena on a check flight necessitated by a change of engine. Weeks was heard from when 520 miles east of Manila; then he disappeared. Search and rescue operations found nothing. No cause for the accident was ever ascertained, and it remains a mystery to this day. Once again, the official news release identified the lost aircraft as an SR-71 and security was maintained.

A few days afterwards the two remaining planes on Okinawa flew to the US and were stored with the remainder of the family.

Final Blackbird Ceremony

In summary: the program lasted just over ten years, from its first inception in 1957 through first flights in 1962 to termination in 1968. Lockheed produced 15 *"OXCARTS,"* three YF-12-A's, and 31 SR-71's. Five *"OXCARTS"* were lost in accidents; two pilots were killed, and two had narrow escapes. In addition, two F-101 chase planes were lost with their Air Force pilots during *"OXCART'S"* testing phase.

The main objective of the program was to create a reconnaissance aircraft of unprecedented speed, range, and altitude capability - was triumphantly achieved. It may well be, however, that the most important aspects of the effort lay in its by-products - the notable advances in aerodynamic design, engine performance, cameras, electronic countermeasures, pilot life support systems, antiradar devices, and above all in milling, machining, and shaping titanium. Altogether it was a pioneering accomplishment.

In a final ceremony at the Nevada base on 26 June 1968, Vice Admiral Rufus L. Taylor, Deputy Director of Central Intelligence, presented the CIA Intelligence Star for valor to pilots Kenneth S. Collins, Ronald L. Layton, Francis J. Murray, Dennis B. Sullivan, and Mele Vojvodich for participation in the *"BLACK SHIELD"* operation. The posthumous award to pilot Jack W. Weeks was accepted by his widow. The United States Air Force Legion of Merit was presented to Colonel Slater and his Deputy, Colonel Maynard N. Amundson. The Air Force Outstanding Unit Award was presented to the members of the Detachment (1129th Special Activities Squadron, Detachment 1) and the USAF supporting units.

Wives of the pilots were present and learned for the first time of the activities in which their husbands had been involved. Kelly Johnson was a guest speaker at the ceremony and lamented in moving words the end of an enterprise, which had marked his most outstanding achievement in aircraft design. His own awards had already been received: The President's Medal of Freedom in 1964, and on 10 February 1966, the National Medal of Science, from President Johnson, for his contributions to aerospace science and to the national security.

SR-71 Program Termination (156)

The U.S. Air Force (USAF) retired its fleet of SR-71s on Jan. 26, 1990, because of: 1) Largely due to Pentagon politics 2) Decreasing defense budget, 3) High costs of operation and 4) Availability of sophisticated spy satellites.

ITEK made the same model optical bar cameras for the U2, SR-71's and satellites so their photos are similar.

Image Taken by Satellite Photography of Osama bin Laden's Compound in the Pakistani City of Abbottabad Made by the CIA.

Proponents of the Blackbird program believed a mistake had been made with its withdrawal from service and fought tooth and nail for its return. With enthusiasts around the world, and more importantly in Congress, the SR-71 was a hard program to kill. SR-71 proponents prevailed and 100 million dollars was allocated by Congress in 1994 to return three SR-71s to Air Force service. However, the fight to end their service wasn't over. In 1996 the SR-71's were

153

grounded again by Deputy Defense Secretary John White, but funding was returned the same year.

The program was ultimately canceled by President Clinton with a line-item veto in 1997. A Supreme Court ruling determined that the line-item veto was unconstitutional, but the funds were never issued. The final shut down of the United States Air Force SR-71 program occurred on Jun 30th, 1999, at Edwards AFB. All remaining SR-71s were transferred to NASA. The final SR-71 flight was made by 61-7980 on October 9th in 1999 at the Edwards AFB open house air show.

Launching a Satellite Cost More Than Operating a Fleet of Three "Blackbirds" for ~Nine Years

Launching a single satellite with an ITEK optical bar camera into space will cost about $390 million. [165] Bringing back an existing fleet of three "*Blackbirds*" will cost $45 million the first year, including startup cost, and a lesser amount for the second and following years ($40 million).

Less than two years after termination of the SR-71 program, and in the immediate aftermath of the 9/11 attacks on the New York twin towers, on the 13th of September, 2001, the Pentagon asked if the SR-71 could be brought back. Not only was the answer Yes, but the now-scattered Blackbird community could recover and provide intelligence products within 60 to 90 days at a cost of 45 million dollars for startup and one year of operations. The proposal went on to outline that year two costs would be reduced to 40 million dollars.

The role for the SR-71 Blackbird in the "*Global War On Terror*" was reported by Major William Michael Zimmerman, SR-71 Reactivation Program Manager, to be wide-area mapping in addition to the ongoing strategic deterrent of making non-lethal shows of force in the form of sonic booms over or near enemy territory as directed by our elected leaders and combatant commanders.

From the beginning of the program upstarts and shutdowns in the 1990s, five SR-71 Blackbirds were retained between NASA and the USAF, and all were based at Edwards AFB. Those included SR-71A 61-7968, which was prepped for a return to service, but kept in storage and not flown at all after February 12th, 1990. Ultimately, It was sent to the Virginia Aviation Museum in October 1999. Three remain property of Lockheed, and three have been kept by NASA to study aerodynamics, propulsion, structures, thermal protection materials, and instrumentation.

A total of four SR-71s were flown by the Air Force and NASA at different times as the program evolved in the 1990s. 61-7980 stayed with NASA as #844 from 1990 on, 61-7967 was reactivated by the Air Force in 1995 from storage, and 61-7971 went to NASA as was #832 in 1990, but was given back to the Air Force in 1995. The first built and last surviving of two SR-71B dual front cockpit trainers, 61-7956, had stayed active at Edwards AFB supporting SR-71 flight training for both NASA (as #831) and Air Force aircrews. In early July 1999, all four flyable Blackbirds were transferred to NASA.

The four remaining flyable SR-71 Blackbirds were disposed of by the end of 2003. 61-7980 stayed at Edwards AFB and was moved to a display near the Armstrong Flight Research Center in March of 2002. The other Blackbirds required shipping to their final resting places, which necessitated their wings being sawed off by Worldwide Aircraft Recovery.

All tooling used to produce the SR-71 was ordered destroyed by the pentagon. The Blackbird community largely considers SR-71B 61-7956's dismantling the conclusive end of the Blackbird program. With no trainer available to keep crews proficient, any hope of a return to service was lost.

Possible Replacement for the SR-71

Both Lockheed and Northrup Grumman are presently working prototypes of a concept to replace the void left by canceling the SR-71 program.

Lockheed's SR-72

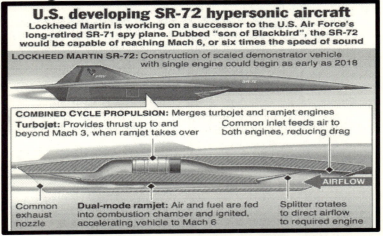

Northrup's RQ-180

Lockheed and Northrup Grumman Are Both Working an Unmanned SR-71 Replacement

U.S. developing SR-72 hypersonic aircraft

Lockheed Martin is working on a successor to the U.S. Air Force's long-retired SR-71 spy plane. Dubbed "son of Blackbird", the SR-72 would be capable of reaching Mach 6, or six times the speed of sound

LOCKHEED MARTIN SR-72: Construction of scaled demonstrator vehicle with single engine could begin as early as 2018

COMBINED CYCLE PROPULSION: Merges turbojet and ramjet engines

Turbojet: Provides thrust up to and beyond Mach 3, when ramjet takes over

Common inlet feeds air to both engines, reducing drag

AIRFLOW

Common exhaust nozzle

Dual-mode ramjet: Air and fuel are fed into combustion chamber and ignited, accelerating vehicle to Mach 6

Splitter rotates to direct airflow to required engine

Lockheed's Proposed SR-72

Lockheed is proposing a Mach # = 6.0 [163] and Northrup Grumman is proposing the RQ-180. [164] Both versions are unmanned. Boeing is also working a Mach 5.0 replacement for the SR-71 ("*Waverider*").

Appendix

Timeline of the SR 71 and Area 51 ⁽¹⁵⁵⁾

The following SR-71 timeline is a compilation of important dates pulled from many sources.

1910 February/27 - Clarence Leonard "*Kelly*" Johnson is born in Ishpeming Michigan.

1916 - The first American military reconnaissance flight ever flown. It was flown in a Curtiss Flyer over France by the 9th Wing. The 9th Wing later became the unit to fly SR-71 missions from its home base of Beale Air Force Base California and it's various operational units. The most notable of these was Detachment at Kadena Air Base in Okinawa.

1933 - Clarence L. "*Kelly*" Johnson joins Lockheed Aircraft Corporation as a fledgling Engineer. He excels at aircraft design and was the principal designer and builder of the P-38 Lightning. The P-38 was the most maneuverable propeller driven fighter in World War II.

1943 - The United States watches as the first German jet fighters appear in the war over Europe. The War Department turns to Kelly Johnson to build a jet fighter prototype. Kelly declares that he can design and build a new jet fighter aircraft, the XP-80, in just 180 days. The challenge to Lockheed management is called and he is allowed to handpick 22 Engineers and a number of mechanics. He sets up shop in a small assembly shed on the Lockheed facility in Burbank California. To get the needed room and to save money, Kelly sets up a big circus tent for his operation. They worked in wartime total secrecy, with total autonomy and produce the first operational American jet fighter aircraft, the P-80 Shooting Star in just 143 days. It was June 1943 and the legendary

"*Skunk Works*" was born. Kelly Johnson's motto was, "*Be Quick, Be Quiet, Be on Time*".

The official name of the "*Skunk Works*" was The Advanced Design Projects Office. The nick name "*Skunk Works*" was taken from the Li'l Abner cartoon strip by Al Capp. In the cartoon strip, the character Injun Joe, operated the "*Dogpatch Kickapoo Joy Juice Factory*" (a moonshine still) in the local woods. Injun Joe would toss old worn shoes, dead skunks, etc. into his smoldering vat to make the legendary Kickapoo Joy Juice. Injun Joe's operation was a super secret affair and was known in the cartoon strip as the "*Skunk Works*" because of the foul smell it gave off. Nobody knows for certain, but, it was rumored that the nickname Skunk Works became popular after one of the Kelly's Engineers answered the phone one day, "*The Skunk Works - may I help you*"?

1947 - The CIA is created by the National Security Act After World War II, the United States is conducting secret reconnaissance over flights of the Soviet Union with B-57's. The US was worried about the Soviet military and desperately wanted to know what was going on. These reconnaissance flights are not deep penetration flights. They only covered the border areas over Soviet space. They were, however, vulnerable to Soviet countermeasures. Until the development of the U-2 and its first use in 1956, hundreds of airmen were lost when their bombers were shot down over the Soviet Union. The United States kept this secret because they didn't want to admit to these operations. The Soviet Union kept it a secret because they didn't want to admit that they could be over flown with such ease.

1948 - Camp Beale is acquired by the new United States Air Force.

1953 - President Eisenhower proposed to Khrushchev to allow unfettered over flights by both nations to photograph military installations as a way to stabilize the situation.

When Khrushchev refused, Eisenhower gave the green light for the development of a reconnaissance aircraft capable of over flights of the Soviet Union above the range of Soviet counter measures. Eisenhower states; *"I think our country needs this kind of information and I approve this project of reconnaissance flights. But I am warning you, one of these days one of these planes is going to be caught. When that happens we're going to have a hell of a problem on our hands."* Eisenhower categorically refused the possibility of letting someone from the US Air Force fly one of the aircraft. Eisenhower states; *"If such an aircraft was to be shot down whilst it was flying over the Soviet Union, I'd prefer it to be a civilian aircraft with a civilian pilot, the provocation would then be slightly less in the eyes of the* Communists..."

1953/March - CIA issues a specification for a reconnaissance aircraft capable of 70,000 feet and a range of 1,750 miles. This leads to a contract with the Lockheed *"Skunk Works"* to develop an aircraft we know as the U-2. The U-2 program was code named *"ANGEL"* at the *"Skunk Works."*

1954 - CIA Director, Allen Dulles, appointed Richard M. Bissell as his special assistant for planning and coordination to oversee the U-2 program. The CIA used the code name *"PROJECT AQUATONE"*. To help mislead the Communist Intelligence Service, the aircraft was designated U signifying '*Utility*' in the US Air Force designation code.

1954/January - The construction of the first few U-2 aircrafts are nearing completion and flight tests will soon begin. Lockheed's chief test pilot Tony LeVier was ordered, by Kelly Johnson, to find a suitable site for secret testing of the U-2.

1954/November - Lockheed chief test pilot Tony LeVier and chief *"Skunk Works"* foreman Dorsey Kammerer set out in a Lockheed owned Beechcraft Bonanza on a secret mission to search for a suitable U-2 test site. They told everyone they were going on a hunting trip in Mexico. They dressed and packed appropriately to keep their hunting trip cover realistic. During their two week mission, they photographed and explored desert areas, which had potential as a test site in southern California, Nevada and Arizona. Groom Lake in Nevada came in as the top choice from hundreds of possible sites. Groom Lake is a dry lake-bed located about 100 miles northwest of Las Vegas, Nevada and just south of Bald Mountain. At that time, there was no highway 375 or the town of Rachel. Groom Lake was located on the Nevada Nuclear test grounds, which had been divided into numbered area grids during atomic bomb testing. Groom Lake was on the grid number 51. This was the infamous Area 51 before it became widely known as "*Area 51*."

1954/December/9 - The CIA signs a contract to buy the first batch of twenty U-2 aircraft.

1955 - Groom Lake begins it's readiness for operations. All work (runways, hangers, quarters, water wells, sewers, etc.) is contracted through the C.L.J. Construction Firm (C.L.J. are the initials of Kelly Johnson). All contracts were paid in cash with funds obtained secretly from the CIA. Kelly would find blank envelops of cash in his home mail-box from time to time and use this to obtain the services needed.

1955/July - Groom Lake flight center is ready for U-2 test flights. Groom Lake was also known as Home Plate, Watertown Strip, Area 51, Paradise Ranch, The Ranch or Dreamland. Watertown Strip was the CIA's semi-official name.

1955/July/24 - The first U-2 was flown in parts to Groom Lake on a C-124 Globemaster. All flights carrying U-2s to Groom Lake were accomplished at night to avoid attention. The C-124s flew to Groom Lake in complete darkness and the runway lights were only turned on at the last few minutes before landing. The C-124 pilots, flying in total darkness, were amazed to suddenly see a runway pop up.

1955/August/4 - First flight of a U-2 (article 341), the pilot was Tony LeVier. The term *"article"* was a Skunk Works designation which was similar to the term "serial number".

1955/October - Tony LeVier leaves Groom Lake (never to return) to become director of flight operations at Lockheed.

1955 - During test flights of the U-2, the then world altitude record of 64,000 feet was routinely broken by thousands of feet. However, that fact was a secret at the time.

1956/May - J-58 engines come under contract at Pratt & Whitney. The Pratt & Whitney J-58 afterburning bypass turbojet engine were used in the SR-71s. The engines were originally intended for Navy aircrafts.

1956/May/7 - National Advisory Committee for Aeronautics (NACA) announces the start of a new research program and a new airplane, the Lockheed U-2. This was the first public acknowledgement of the existence of the U-2. The NACA announcement listed, high altitude research, air turbulence studies, connective cloud tests, wind sheer testing, jet stream research, cosmic rays studies, ozone and water vapor studies. All this research happened much later. The U-2 was a spy plane, the research projects were just a cover story.

1956/June - U-2s declared operational

1956/July/4 - U-2s conduct the first *"Operation Overflight"* out of Weisbaden, West Germany. This mission was an overflight of the Soviet Union. This operation was under the cover designation of 1st Weather Reconnaissance Squadron, Provisional (WRSP-1). Other operational locations followed; WRSP-2 in Incirlik Turkey, WRSP-3 in Atsugi Japan.

1956/July/9 - The NACA makes another announcement about the great research work being conducted with the U-2. It informs the public of the need to conduct these types of research flights overseas. This just another cover story to explain the presence of U-2 in Germany and other locations. Through out 1957, 1958 and 1959 the U-2 regularly over flew the Soviet Union at a rate of about once per month. The Soviets tried in vain to intercept the U-2 flights. However, they continued to get closer with each attempt. The United States knew that it was only a matter of time before a U-2 would be lost over the Soviet Union.

1956/October/18 - Air Force cancels the design efforts of the REX engine hydrogen <u>fuel study</u>. This engine design was considered for the SR-71.

1957/Fall - CIA arranges with Skunk Works to study how speed and altitude effect the possibility of being shot down. The results of this study concluded that supersonic speed when combined with altitude and low radar cross section, greatly reduced the chances of detection and vulnerability to counter measures.

1957/Winter - The CIA asks Lockheed and Convair to propose high speed and high altitude designs.

1957/December/24 - First J-58 engine test run.

1958 - US is becoming more concerned that the Soviets would soon be able to shoot down a U-2.

1958/April - Kelly Johnson proposes to build an aircraft that will fly 60% faster than the maximum dash capability of the top jet fighter and 5 miles higher than the U-2.

1958/April/21 - First mention of project "*ARCHANGEL*" in Kelly Johnson's dairy. Since the new project was to

162

replace the U-2 with a code name ANGEL, "*ARCHANGEL*" was a natural code name.

1958/July/23 - Kelly presents the Lockheed design concepts to the Land Advisory Committee.

1958/August/27 - Beale Air Force Base is fully operational under the Strategic Air Command with newly built 12,000 foot runways.

1958/September - Several "*ARCHANGEL*" deign variations are under consideration at the Skunk Works. Lockheed's first "*Blackbird*" on the design board was the A-1. As the design considerations progressed, they were coded A-2, A-3, A-4, etc.

1958/November - The Land Advisory Committee reviews Lockheed's A-3 design and the Convair FISH proposal. The committee recommends and the CIA obtains $100 million to fund detailed designs and to build 12 aircraft. Code named "*GUSTO*".

1958/December - CIA requests funding for a Mach 3+ reconnaissance aircraft program.

1959/May - Lockheed design numbering is up to A-11.

1959/July/20 - The President is briefed on the current designs and gives final approval for a Mach 3+ program to get underway.

1959/August/29 - Lockheed and Convair submit proposals for Mach 3 reconnaissance aircraft.

1959/September/3 - The CIA terminated project "*GUSTO*" and asks Lockheed to develop a U-2 follow-on aircraft under the CIA code name. The CIA authorizes

Lockheed to proceed with anti-radar studies, aerodynamic structural tests and Engineering designs.

1959/September/14 - CIA awards first research contract to Lockheed. Lockheed works on the program under the Lockheed code name of *"ARCHANGEL"*.

1959/November - Lockheed builds a full sized mock-up of the design at that time. It was secretly trailered to Groom Lake. It was hoisted on the top of a pylon and viewed from various angles with radar. From this testing new features were added to reduce the radar image, including the distinctive chine feature. After some modifications the designation is changed from A-11 to A-12. The CIA contracts with Pratt & Whitney to build and test an initial three J-58 engines to be ready in early 1961 - Perkin-Elmer is selected as the primary camera supplier with Eastman-Kodak to build a backup design. Minneapolis-Honeywell is selected to develop the inertial navigation system and the automatic flight control system. Firewell and the David Clark Corporations became the primary suppliers of the pilot equipment and the associated life support systems.

1960 - Some time in the early 1960s, the highly classified National Reconnaissance Office (NRO) was created. Its task was to combine reconnaissance operations at the CIA and Defense Department. The existence of the NRO was secret until 1992 when its general mission was made public. The SR-71 was one of the many assets available to the NRO. In 1960, Groom Lake began being referred to as *"Area 51."* Groom Lake was part of a large adjoining atomic test site. During the days of the atomic testing, the test site was divided up into nondescript numbered areas and Groom Lake just happened to be located in the section known as *"Area 51."*

1960/January/26 - CIA orders an initial five A-12 *"OXCART"* aircraft

1960/February - Lockheed begins its search for 24 pilots for the A-12. Test pilot Louis W. Schalk joins the program and starts by assisting with cockpit layout. Pilots were to be qualified in high performance fighter aircraft, 25-40 years old, and to be able fit into the A-12s cockpit, under 6 feet tall and under 175 pounds. The CIA also had numerous emotional stability and motivational requirements.

1960/February/11 - CIA signs the contract, which ordered a full twelve *"OXCART"* aircraft.

1960/May/1 - Francis Gary Powers, shot down over the Soviet Union near Sverdlovsk, in a CIA operated U-2, article number 360. The flight originated from Peshawar Pakistan and was to end by landing at Bodo, Norway. Powers was brought down by an improved Soviet SA-2 missile.

1960/September - Additions to Groom Lake are under construction to accommodate the A-12s. Lockheed supplied a C-47 shuttle from it's Burbank plant to Groom Lake. A D-18 was chartered to shuttle from Las Vegas. The law in Nevada required any contractors to be named if working/staying in the State for more than 48 hours. Since security did not permit release of the names, and, since Government employees were exempt from this State requirement, all contractors received appointments as Government consultants.

1960/September/7 through November 15 - New runway constructed at Groom Lake.

1960/September - Kelly proposes to build a long range, very high speed interceptor to address a perceived Soviet threat.

1960/October - Letter sent to Lockheed to build and test three AF-12 interceptors. Project code name *"KEDLOCK"*.

1961/January - Kelly Johnson proposes an RS-12 dual-role strategic reconnaissance bomber. This idea doesn't go far due to an Air Force interest in the B-70 program.

1961/May/31 - A forward fuselage mockup of an AF-12 was completed and inspected by an Air Force group.

1961/June - Wind tunnel tests of the AF-12 design revealed that the revised A-12 nose and cockpit configuration caused directional stability problems at high Mach. In an effort to solve this, a large folding ventral stabilizer was added under the aft fuselage, and a small, fixed ventral fin was added under each engine. This gave the AF-12 a very distinctive appearance.

A thorough survey of the highway route from Burbank to Groom Lake was made to ascertain the hazards and problems of moving the A-12s to Groom Lake. Planned package measured 35 feet wide and 105 feet long. Obstructing road signs had to be removed, trees trimmed and some roadsides leveled. Arrangements were made with police authorities and local officials.

1961/July/5 - General Curtis LeMay of the Air Force, expresses interest in a bomber version of the A-12. The Q-bay located behind the cockpits (later the ANS bay) was envisioned as the bomb bay.

1961/November - An initial five CIA pilots were selected. The search for other pilots continued. The final list of A-12 CIA pilots was: William L. Skliar, Kenneth S. Collins, Walter R. Ray, Lon Walter, Mele Vojvodich Jr, Jack W. Weeks, Ronald *"Jack"* Layton, Dennis B. Sullivan David P. Young, Francis J. Murray, & Russell Scott.
USAF Colonel Robert J. Holbury was named commander of the Groom Lake facility.

1962 - Fuel tank farm completed and ready at Groom Lake with a capacity of 1,320,000 gallons.

1962/January - Agreement was reached with the Federal Aviation Agency that expanded the restricted airspace in the vicinity of Groom Lake to preserve and enhance security. Selected FAA air traffic controllers were cleared for the *"OXCART"* project to ensure they did not talk about what they might see. The North American Air Defense Command (NORAD) established procedures to prevent their radar stations from reporting the appearance of high performance aircraft on their radar scopes.

Special tank farms were installed in California, at Eielson AFB Alaska, Thule AB Greenland, Kadena AB Okinawa and Adana Turkey. Very small detachments of technicians were deployed at these facilitates to maintain the specially refined fuel which was reserved for the project. A-12 (924), CIA Article #121 (the first *"Blackbird"*) received its final tests and checkouts at the Lockheed Burbank plant (Skunk Works).

1962/February/10 - Francis Gary Powers is released from Soviet prison and exchanged for a KGB Agent, Rudolf Abel.

1962/February/26 - A-12 (924) is disassembled and placed in a specially designed trailer (costing $100,000) 105 feet long and 35 feet wide for transport to Groom Lake.

1962/February/28 - The first A-12 (924) arrives at Groom Lake.

1962/Spring - Support aircraft and equipment began arriving at Groom Lake.

1962/April - Lockheed begins working on concepts that would later become the SR-71.

1962/April/24 - First A-12 (924) engine test runs completed, high speed taxi tests. Pilot Lou Schalk accidental lifts off for a few seconds (first actual flight but not considered official).

1962/April/26 - First true A-12 (924) flight. Pilot Lou Schalk. 33 minutes, less than 300 knots. At Groom Lake. "Blackbird"s fly!

1962/April/30 - "*OXCARTS*" first "*official*" flight, A-12 (924). Witnessed by a number of CIA and Air Force representatives. Pilot Lou Schalk. 340 knots, 30,000 feet, 59 minutes. This flight was just under one year later than originally planned. Bill Park joins the pilot program.

1962/May/2 or 4 – An "*OXCART*" broke the sound barrier for the first time at Mach 1.1 using A-12 (924). Then Director of the CIA, John McCone sent a telegram of congratulation to Kelly Johnson. 1962/May - Promotional fights for McNamara were launched. Edwards AFB to Orlando FL (1 hour 28 minutes). San Diego CA to Savannah Beach GA (59 minutes).

1962/June/13 - SR-71 mock-up reviewed by Air Force officials.

1962/June/26 - Second A-12 (925) arrives at Groom Lake.

1962/July/30 - J-58 completes pre-flight testing.

1962/Summer - Lockheed working simultaneously on the A-12 and the AF-12 programs.

1962/August - Third A-12 (926) arrives at Groom Lake. Jim Eastman joins the pilot program. A-12 (925) first flight at Groom Lake. CIA letter of intent for $1 million for the YF-12 is sent to Lockheed.

1962/October/5 - Start of engine change from J-75 to J-58. A-12 flights with one J-75 and one J-58 engine.

1962/October/10 - The CIA authorized Lockheed to study a new Drone program code named "*Tagboard*". Within the Skunk Works, the drone was known as Q-12. As work progressed it was given the D-21 designation. For the "Tagboard" project, Lockheed built two M-21 aircraft. The M-21 was not a modified A-12, but it did have only a few differences from the A-12. The D-21 stood for "*daughter*" and the M-21 stood for "*mother*". The 21 designation was simply 12 reversed to avoid confusion.

1962/October/14 - U2 flight over Cuba discovers Soviet ballistic missile base.

1962/October/27 - A U2 was shot down by a SAM over Cuba. The pilot, Rudolph Anderson was killed. The program goes into high gear.

1962/November - The only A-12 trainer arrives at Groom Lake. A-12 (927) was a two seater version intended for pilot training. The A-12B trainer was known as "*The Titanium Goose.*"

1962/December/3 - By the end of 1962, only two A-12s were engaged in flight tests. Full test speeds could not be reached since the J-58 engines were not fully available and were experiencing problems. CIA Director, McCone wrote to the President of United Aircraft Corporation (the parent company of Pratt & Whitney) and made a clear case by stating "*I have been advised that the J-58 engine deliveries have been delayed again due to engine control problems. . . by the end of the year it appears we will have barely enough J-58 engines to support the flight test program adequately. . . Furthermore, due to various engine difficulties we have not yet reached design speed and altitude. Engine thrust and fuel consumption deficiencies at present prevent sustained flight at design conditions which is so necessary to complete development*". By the end of January 1963, ten engines were available and the first flight with two J-58 engines occurred on January 15.

1962/December/7 - A full scale mock-up of the proposed D-21 drone was completed.

1962/December/17 - The 5th A-12 (928) arrives at Groom Lake. The Air Force expresses an interest in obtaining reconnaissance versions of the *"Blackbird"*. Lockheed obtains a USAF contract to build six SR-71s.

1962/December/28 - Began weapons system developments for the AF-12. Kelly Johnson obtained approval to design a Mach 3 *"Blackbird"* fighter / bomber

1963/January - First flight of the A-12 (927) trainer, the Titanium Goose. Robert Gilliland joins the pilot program. Ten J-58 engines arrive at Groom Lake. All A-12s were fitted with J-58 engines and the flight test program goes to three-shift work days.

1963/January/15 - First A-12 flight with duel J-58 engines. At speeds of Mach 2.4-2.8 the aircraft experienced such severe roughness that it was looking as if the program could not move forward. The trouble was diagnosed as being in the air inlet system of the engines. After a considerable period of experimentation, the problem was solved.

1963/February/18 - Air Force authorizes the initial construction of the first six SR-71s. These aircrafts were designated R-12s. The project code name was *"SENIOR CROWN"*.

1963/May/24 - First loss of a *"Blackbird"* A-12 (926) was due to instrument failure. Pilot Ken Collins ejected and was unharmed. The crash occurred 14 miles south of Wendover, Utah. The wreckage was recovered in two days. Local residents signed secrecy agreements and the press was told that an F-105 had crashed.

1963/May/31 - The mockup of the AF-12 (YF-12) is shown to the USAF.

1963/June/13 - Initial mockup review of the R-12 (SR-71) by the USAF.

1963/July - First AF-12 was trucked to Groom Lake.

1963/July/1 - Air Force authorizes the construction of an additional 25 SR-71s.

1963/July/20 - First A-12 Mach 3 flight. Pilot Lou Schalk.

1963/August - Production of the D-21 drones begins.

1963/August/7 - First AF-12 (934) test flight. Pilot James Eastham.

1963/November/ November/22 - President Kennedy assassinated.

1963/November/29 - President Johnson called a National Security Council meeting to discuss whether to, or how to, release the technological aspects of the program.

1963/November - The design speed of Mach 3.2 was achieved by an A-12. Altitude 78,000 feet.

1963/December/11 - Final Air Force review of R-12 (SR-71).

1963/December/17 - A-12 (928) arrives at Groom Lake.

1963/December - Nine A-12s are in Service. The YF-12s (AF-12s) were fully ready for test launches of the GAR-9 air-to-air missiles.

1964/February - The B-58 testing of the GAR-9 air-to-air missile was canceled.

1964/February/4 - A-12 (924) sustained flight at Mach 3+ and altitude. Pilot James Easthem reached Mach 3.3 at 83,000 feet for just over 10 minutes. Aircraft heated to 800 F. Wiring insulation was burned and the aircraft was almost lost. All A-12s grounded for 6 weeks while Lockheed replaced all wiring in all the A-12s.

1964/February/7 - First photo of a YF-12 released. Aircraft 934.

1964/February/29 - President Johnson announced, "*The United States has successfully developed an advanced experimental jet aircraft, the A-11, which has been tested in sustained flight at more than 2,000 mph and at altitudes in excess of 70,000 feet. The performance of the A-11 far exceeds that of any other aircraft in the world today. The development of this aircraft has been made possible by major advances in aircraft technology of great significance to both military and commercial applications. Several A-11 aircraft are now being flight tested at Edwards AFB in California... The A-11 aircraft now at Edwards AFB are undergoing extensive tests to determine their capabilities as long-range interceptors.*" The proper designation of the A-11s that President Johnson referred to was the AF-12. The A-11 reference was used to mislead intelligence sources. Also, there were no "*Blackbirds*" at Edwards AFB at that time. Following the Presidents announcement, the AF-12 officially was changed to YF-12A. The YF-12 program became an overt operation while the A-12 was to remain a black program at Groom Lake.

1964/March - Construction on the first six R-12s (SR-71) well underway.

1964/March/13 - YF-12 (936) first flight by Jim Eastman. The Air Force designates the Lockheed R-12 as RS-71. This was the follow on number of the RS-70 version of the XB-70.

1964/April/1 - First M-21 flight (940).

1964/April/16 - The first AIM-47A air-to-air missile is fired from a YF-12.

1964/June - Final A-12 (939) Article 133, delivered to Groom Lake.

1964/June/19 - The first fit test of a D-21 to a M-21 (940) at the Skunk Works.

1964/July/9 - Pilot Bill Park took A-12 (939) to a record altitude of 96,250 feet. The A-12 crashed on landing at Groom Lake due to an outboard aileron servo valve that was stuck. Pilot Bill Park ejected safely.

1964/July/25 - President Johnson publicly revealed the existence of a new Air Force reconnaissance aircraft, which he called the SR-71 instead of RS-71. The Air Force decided that it was easier to re-number the aircraft SR-71 than to correct the President. Thus we all know the aircraft as the SR-71 to this day.

1964/August/12 - The Air Force asked Lockheed to come up with a program to use an YF-12A to publicly break records. This was finally accomplished on May 1, 1965.

1964/October - Construction on the first SR-71 (950), completed.

1964/October/29 - First SR-71 (950) transported to the Palmdale test facility by specially design trailer. Air Force Plant 42, Site 2, Palmdale.

1964/December/7 - Beale Air Force Base, California, announced as the home base for SR-71s. Beale AFB was the home base of the SR-71 throughout its entire career.

1964/December/22 - First captive flight test of an M-21 (940) and a D-21 drone. Pilot Bill Park. First flight of an SR-71 (950) at Palmdale CA. Pilot Robert J. Gilliland. RSO was an seat empty.

1964/December - Eleven A-12s flying. Three YF-12s flying. Two M-21s flying. One SR-71 flying.

1965/January/1 - The 4200th Strategic Reconnaissance Wing activated at Beale AFB. Later (25 June 1966) it was changed to 9th Strategic Reconnaissance Wing.

1965/January/9 - Pilot Jim Eastham sustained Mach 3.23 for 5 minutes in a YF-12A (934).

1965/January/27 - A-12 flown for 1 hour and 40 minutes above Mach 3.1 for a distance of 3,000 miles.

1965/May/14 - The Air Force funded $500,000 to continue Engineering work on the F-12B (the operational configuration of the YF-12A.

1965/August/5 - Director of the National Security Agency, General Marshall S. Carter, directed operational readiness for flights over Cuba. Code named "*SKYLARK*". Due to priorities in Southeast Asia, "*SKYLARK*" was never launched.

1965/September/28 - An AIM-47 missile was fired from a YF-12A at Mach 3.2 flying at 75,000 feet. The missile missed its intended target 36 miles away flying at 40,000 feet by less than 7 feet.

1965/November/20 - Four A-12 aircraft selected to support operation "*BLACK SHIELD*". Aircraft 930, 931,932, 934 were selected. 931 remained at Groom Lake as backup. The actual deployment did not take place until May 22, 1967. Bill Park flew an A-12 at Mach 3.29 and an altitude of 90,000 feet with a sustained flight time above Mach 3.2 of 1 hour 14 minutes.

1965/November – Program declared operational.

1966/January/7 - The Air Force took delivery of its first SR-71. Aircraft 956 trainer, Pilot Doug Nelson (4200th SRW, Wing Commander) and instructor pilot Raymond Haupy. Arrived at Beale AFB CA.

1966/January/25 - SR-71 (952) came apart at Mach 3.17 and 80,000 feet due to pitch up accident. Pilot Bill Weaver and RSO Jim Zwayer ejected. Jim Zwayer was killed. Lost north of Tucumcary, NM.

1966/March/5 - First successful launch of the Drone (#503) from M-21 (941). *"Blackbird"* pilot Bill Park. Takeoff from Groom Lake. Launched Drone over Pacific Ocean at 80,000 feet, Mach 3.2. Successful launch. Drone traveled 150 miles and ran out of fuel. Launch Control Officer was Heith Beswick.

1966/April/4 - First mission ready SR-71 (958) delivered to the Air Force at Beale AFB.

1966/April/25 - Two YF-12 were flown to Eglin AFB in Florida for firing trials. On the same day Jim Eastham fired an unarmed AIM-47 against a QB-47 flying 60,000 feet below. The missile passed through the QB-47s horizontal stabilizer. The YF-12s scored an impressive 6 hits out of 7 attempts. The single miss was attributed to missile gyro defects.

1966/April/27 - Second successful launch of the *"Tagboard"* Drone (#506) from M-21 (941). *"Blackbird"* pilot Bill Park. Takeoff from Groom Lake. Launched Drone over Pacific Ocean at 80,000 feet, Mach 3.3. Successful launch. Drone traveled 1120 miles, Drone was lost due to hydraulic pump failure. Launch Control Officer was Ray Torrick.

1966/April/29 - 15 more D-21s are ordered.

1966/June/16 - Third test flight launch of the *"Tagboard"* Drone (#505). Bill Park pilot, Keith Beswick in back seat as launch operator. Launched Drone over Pacific Ocean. Successful launch. Drone traveled 1600 miles making eight programmed turns and collecting photographs at 92,000 feet and 4,000+ MPH. Drone did not eject the film package due to electronic failure.

1966/June/25 - The 4200th Strategic Reconnaissance Wing it was changed to 9th Strategic Reconnaissance Wing. The 9th Strategic Reconnaissance Wing was organized as the unit to fly the SR-71.

1966/July/30 - Fourth test flight launch of the *"Tagboard"* Drone (#504) from M-21 (941). Bill Park Pilot, Ray Torrick Launch Control Officer. Launched Drone at Mach 3.25 over Pacific Ocean. Drone collides with the *"Blackbird"* causing it to spin wildly out of control. Bill and Ray both eject. Bill was picked up in a life raft 150 miles at sea. Ray's pressure suit was torn during the ejection and filled his pressure suit with sea water and he drowned before rescue teams could arrive.

1966/August - The M-21/D-21 program terminated. The D-21 drones would soon be modified for launch from a B-52. The B-52s of Beale AFB were used in this program code named *"SENIOR BOWL"*. Fewer than 5 B-52/D-21 operational flights took place.

1966/August/14 - YF-12 (934) is written off after a landing accident at Edwards AFB. The rear of this YF-12 was used to build 61-7981, an SR-71C, which became known as *"The Bastard"*. This SR-71C is on display at Hill AFB Museum, Utah.

1966/December/12 - A Bureau of the Budget meeting was held to vote on three alternatives to continuing with both the *"SENIOR CROWN"* programs. The final vote favored the termination of the program in January 1968, assuming an operational readiness date of September 1967 for the SR- 71's, and assigning all missions to the SR-71 fleet.

1966/December/21 - Longest flight of a A-12 was flown by Bill Park. Lasted just under 6 hours and covered 10,198 miles. This mission was used to demonstrate the A-12s capabilities to support the *"BLACK SHIELD"* project in Okinawa, Japan.

1966/December/28 - President Johnson approves the termination of the program by 1 June 1968 (the A-12 program of the CIA).

1967/January/5 - A-12 (928) was lost near Callente, Nevada. The aircraft ran out of fuel (due to a faulty fuel gauge) and crashed while on approach to Groom Dry Lake. CIA pilot Walt Ray ejected but did not survive due to a failure in his seat. He was found still strapped into the seat.

1967/January/10 - SR-71 (950), lost during wet runway brake testing at Edwards AFB. Pilot Art Peterson survived. The CIA informs the Department of Defense the A-12s would gradually be placed in storage with the process to be completed by the end of January 1967. This was later changed to allow some operational missions of the A-12 over Southeast Asia.

1967/April/13 -SR-71 (966) was lost. Pilot Earle Boone and RSO Butch Sheffield survived.

1967/April/17 - An SR-71 made the longest Mach 3 flight in history. The flight was over 14,000 miles. Pilot Robert L. Stephens (the Silver Fox), RSO Kenneth D. Hurley.

1967/May - The National Security Council was briefed that North Vietnam was about to receive surface-to surface ballistic missiles. The A-12s were considered the best choice to obtain conformation of these missiles. President Johnson approved the planned use of A-12s from Kadena AFB on Okinawa.

1967/May/17 - The notice to deploy to Kadena AFB arrives at Groom Lake.

1967/May/22 - Mele Vojvodich flew an A-12 (937) non-stop from Groom Lake to Kadena in 6 hours and 6 minutes, 6,873 miles. Due to the secrecy of the *"BLACK SHIELD"* operations, this flight was not recognized as a new transpacific speed record.

1967/May/24 - Jack Layton flew A-12 (930) non-stop from Groom Lake to Kadena in 5 hours and 55 minutes.

1967/May/26 - Jack Weeks flew A-12 (932) to Kadena. In route he had INS (Inertial Navigation System) and communication problems. He was forced to land at Wake Island. A recovery team arrived, repaired the problems and he arrived at Kadena on May 27.

1967/May/29 - The CIA operation "*BLACK SHIELD*" declared operational at Kadena AFB on Okinawa. CIA operational missions were called "*GIANT SCALE*" missions.

1967/May/31 - First operational mission of an A-12 (937). Pilot Mele Vojvodich. The target was North Vietnam. 70 of the known 190 SAM sites and 9 primary targets were photographed successfully. Flown at Mach 3.1, 80,000 feet, 3 hours 39 minutes.

1967/July/2 - First international flight of an SR-71 (972). During a training mission the ANS (Astronautical Navigation System) failed and the aircraft accidentally flew into Mexico. Pilot Jim Watkins, RSO Dave Dempster.

1967/August - The Air Force decided not to continue the F-12B (YF-12A) program.

1967/October/25 - SR-71 (965) was lost during night training flight following an ANS platform failure. Aircraft crashed near Lovelock Nevada. Pilot Roy St Martin and RSO John Carnochan survived.

1967/October/28 - An A-12 obtains photos of SAM missiles being launched against the A-12.

178

1967/October/30 - A-12 (932) is the first and only *"Blackbird"* ever to sustain flak damage. Flown by Denny Sullivan. At least 6 missiles were fired and confirmed by photography. Pilot witnessed 3 missile detonations behind the A-12. Traveling at Mach 3.1, 84,000 feet. Post flight inspection revealed the minor flak damage.

1967/November/3 - Operation *"NICE GIRL"*, a fly-off pitting A-12s against SR-71s in an effort to demonstrate which aircraft had better performance. An A-12 and a SR-71 flew identical flight paths, separate in time by 1 hour, from north to south roughly above the Mississippi River. The data gathered was evaluated. The photo images of the A-12 were better, but not to the point where information was lost using the SR-71 images. The SR-71 had other equipment, which the A-12 did not have; infrared, side-looking radar and ELINT (electronic intelligence equipment). The data was inconclusive. The A-12s were given a temporary reprieve in late November 1967.

1967/December/28 - A-12 (929) lost due to the newly-installed SAS (Stability Augmentation System) had the connections wired backwards, causing the airplane to lose complete control just seconds after takeoff from Groom Dry Lake; pilot Mele Vojvodich ejected safely at an altitude of 150 feet. Kelly Johnson receives the Medal of Freedom, the highest civilian award.

1968/January/5 - Lockheed receives the formal letter from the Air Force to not purchase the F-12B follow-on program. The USS Pueblo sails on its maiden operational voyage for the east coast of North Korea.

1968/January/11 - SR-71 (957) lost on final approach to Beale AFB due to a total electrical failure. Crashed on landing approach to Beale AFB. The instructor pilot Robert Sower and the student pilot David Fruehauf both ejected safely.

1968/January/23 - USS Pueblo seized by the North Koreans.

1968/January/24 - First A-12 flight over North Korea to observe the USS Pueblo. Pilot Frank Murray.

1968/February/1 - YF-12 program canceled by formal letter from the Air Force.

1968/February/5 - Lockheed ordered to destroy A-12, YF-12 and SR-71 tooling.

1968/February/19 - Second A-12 flight over North Korea

About the Author - Jack Wilson, Retired Chief Engineer of Florida Turbine Technologies

Jack has >50 years of *"hands on"* experience in the design and development of high performance gas turbines for air breathing systems. He started working in 1965 on the SR-71 engine and has been actively involved, as a design engineer and supervisor, in the design, fabrication, verification, and development testing of over twenty different gas turbines, covering a wide range of power requirements. Jack holds 33 patents that solve complex problems and he is now semi-retired and often works his hobbies.

Disruptive Technology LLC, CEO	2015 – 2022
Florida Turbine Technologies, Inc., Chief Engineer	1998 - 2015
Pratt & Whitney, Manager for JSF and F119 Turbines	1996 – 1998
Pratt & Whitney, Design Supervisor (F119 Exhaust Nozzle and Augmentor)	1995 – 1996
Pratt & Whitney, Leader of F100 Compressor Design Group - Engine for F15/F16	1994 – 1995
Pratt & Whitney, Leader of F100 Turbine/ Combustor Design Group - Engine for F15/F16	1990 – 1994
Pratt & Whitney, Senior Design Engineer Aero Engines	1985 – 1990
Pratt & Whitney, Design Project Engineer,	

Mechanical Design	1975 – 1985

Pratt & Whitney, Design Engineer, Design
of Various Turbines   1972 – 1975

Pratt & Whitney, Design Engineer, F100
Turbine/Compressor Group   1971 – 1972

Pratt & Whitney, Design Engineer, Super-
Sonic Engine Transport Group   1970 – 1971

Pratt & Whitney, Design Engineer,
J58 engine for A-12 & SR-71   1965 - 1970

Education: Bachelor of Science in Mechanical
Engineering – North Carolina State University, 1965

Hobbies: Restoring and customizing pre 1950 cars,
woodworking, gardening, fishing, designing, building and
testing a GPS remote controlled robot that will reduce the
weeds, without applying any poisons to our food and
improve our health.

Jack also enjoys writing books and has researched
extensively whether Jesus was and is real. He is 100%
convinced that Jesus was real and has compiled a book
summarizing his conclusions, including which religions
closely follow the Bible. It is available on Amazon.

He is now semi-retired and CEO of "*Disruptive Technology
LLC*," having fun designing and testing a gas turbine
engine that uses only water as a fuel. It emits no harmful
"*Green House*" gas emissions, only water, and no NOx. If it
is installed in a tractor trailer truck, it is predicted to save
>$40K per year in fuel alone, per 100K miles.

If you have any suggested improvements or additional
topics for the next edition of this book, he can be reached
at: banglyphosate@gmail.com

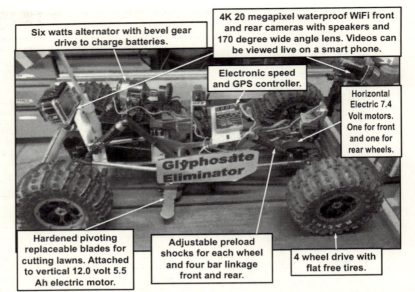

Six watts alternator with bevel gear drive to charge batteries.

4K 20 megapixel waterproof WiFi front and rear cameras with speakers and 170 degree wide angle lens. Videos can be viewed live on a smart phone.

Electronic speed and GPS controller.

Horizontal Electric 7.4 Volt motors. One for front and one for rear wheels.

Glyphosate Eliminator

Hardened pivoting replaceable blades for cutting lawns. Attached to vertical 12.0 volt 5.5 Ah electric motor.

Adjustable preload shocks for each wheel and four bar linkage front and rear.

4 wheel drive with flat free tires.

Jack's GPS Controlled Robot to Eliminate Weeds and Improve People's Health By Eliminating Glyphosate Poison in Our Food (Lawn Mower Version Shown - Easy to Convert to Weed Eater)

Index to Individual Subjects

183

References and More Reading Material

#	References and Locations
1	https://en.wikipedia.org/wiki/Lockheed_SR-71_Blackbird
2	http://www.enginehistory.org/Convention/2005/Presentations/LawPete/SR-71Propulsion1.pdf
3	https://www.iliketowastemytime.com/facts-you-didnt-know-about-sr71-blackbird
4	http://www.freedomsphoenix.com/News/074776-2010-09-01-sr-71-is-faster-than-a-speeding-bullet-and-more.htm
5	https://www.youtube.com/watch?v=6oLFzT7SER8
6	https://en.m.wikipedia.org/wiki/Linear_Aerospike_SR-71_Experiment
7	https://theaviationist.com/2017/12/21/the-blackbird-nasa-used-for-validating-the-sr-71-linear-aerospike-experiment-configuration/
8	https://www.bing.com/images/search?view=detailV2&ccid=8pg7E8Gb&id=5C1E7B8751AC40 7DD15CB71E7D306E6B9C9D10&thid=OIP.8pg7E8GbNMQYGzwGYyEnWAHaF0&mediaurl= https%3a%2f%2fimages.fineartamerica.com%2fimages-medium-large-5%2f2-x-15-launch-from-a-boeing-b-52-nasa.jpg&exph=707&expw=900&q=image+x-15+being+dropped+by+b-52&simid=607993135663546600&ck=9068ACF4FDBCB20E272FE5582450E410&selectedIndex =3&qpvt=image+x-15+being+dropped+by+b-52&FORM=IRPRST&ajaxhist=0
9	https://en.wikipedia.org/wiki/Bell_X-1
10	https://airman.dodlive.mil/2017/07/10/airframe-the-sr-71-blackbird/
11	https://www.warhistoryonline.com/whotube-2/day-n-korea-fired-missile-sr-71_blackbird.html#:~:text=In%20fact%2C%20during%20the%20Vietnam%20War%20over%20 800,a%20Russian%20guided%20missile%20at%20an%20SR-71%20Blackbird.
12	https://militarymachine.com/sr-71-facts/#:~:text=Well%20over%20a%20hundred%20missiles%20were%20shot%20at,from%20r eceiving%20any%20updated%20information%20from%20the%20Blackbird.
13	https://en.wikipedia.org/wiki/Mikoyan_MiG-31
14	https://obtainsurplus.com/blog/u2-sr71-spy-plane-aerial-camera-lens-perkin-elmer-36-f40/
15	https://en.wikipedia.org/wiki/Mikoyan_MiG-31#Specifications_.28MiG-31.29
16	https://armedforces.eu/compare/fighter_aircraft_Mikoyan_MiG-31_vs_McDonnell_Douglas_F-15_Eagle
17	https://www.nasa.gov/centers/armstrong/news/FactSheets/FS-030-DFRC.html
18	https://www.nasa.gov/centers/dryden/pdf/88507main_H-2179.pdf
19	http://www.enginehistory.org/Convention/2005/Presentations/LawPete/SR-71Overview1.pdf
20	http://www.sr-71.org/blackbird/manual/
21	https://theaviationgeekclub.com/remembering-absolute-altitude-record-set-fedotov-mig-25-40-years-ago/
22	https://fighterjetsworld.com/air/mig-31-pilot-explains-how-to-intercept-shoot-down-an-sr-71-spy-plane/9227/
23	https://aviation.stackexchange.com/questions/8028/what-is-the-minimum-turning-radius-of-an-sr-71#:~:text=The%20SR-71%20had%20a%20minimum%20turning%20radius%20at,to%20allow%20for%20much%20lif t%20to%20turn%20with.
24	https://s-media-cache-ak0.pinimg.com/originals/30/75/dc/3075dc613a44a865fea72f5b1795248e.jpg
25	https://www.thefirearmsforum.com/threads/info-on-the-sr-71-blackbird.40606/
26	http://www.u2sr71patches.co.uk/Researchers-Handbook.pdf
27	http://jalopnik.com/5532546/how-to-fly-an-sr-71-blackbird/
28	https://www.businessinsider.com/11-photos-that-show-how-stunning-the-sr-71-blackbird-was-2015-1

#	References and Locations
29	https://www.bing.com/images/search?view=detailV2&ccid=DMHMLQGM&id=207F7BA51693AB7C732E26BEB487DE58EE3BBE33&thid=OIP.DMHMLQGMOSF6NFJg143wQAHaFl&mediaurl=http%3a%2f%2fstatic5.businessinsider.com%2fimage%2f54c11b1e6da811f63bcc6d54-800-603%2flockheed+martin+blackbird+sr+71+cockpit.jpg&exph=603&expw=800&q=sr+71+cockpit+image&simid=608011754335701577&ck=80774138A4BE9976D373038E0B4516F2&selectedIndex=0&qpvt=sr+71+cockpit+image&FORM=IRPRST&ajaxhist=0
30	https://www.sr-71.org/blackbird/sr-71/
31	https://airrefuelingarchive.wordpress.com/category/sr-71/
32	https://airrefuelingarchive.wordpress.com/2016/01/10/sr-71-refueling-pictures/
33	https://www.nasa.gov/centers/dryden/pdf/88507main_H-2179.pdf
34	https://www.bing.com/images/search?view=detailV2&ccid=I%2BYqRxzT&id=A0DB3A1034220E0C3CC309A03F005B588B8BDC64&thid=OIP.I-YqRxzTSpM6PrF5W1BqUwHaHc&mediaurl=https%3A%2F%2Fthumbs.dreamstime.com%2Fb%2Fearth-rising-sun-4320450.jpg&exph=804&expw=800&q=images+sr-71+view+at+80%2c000+feet&simid=608048068319905176&ck=FF87E3CFD180016D9B2DF12194BC5908&selectedindex=8&qpvt=images+sr-71+view+at+80%2c000+feet&form=IRPRST&ajaxhist=0&pivotparams=insightsToken%3Dccid_AjUy2v%252F4*cp_19E5B8CA53960EA49FBFC0577F913E78*mid_39F6DFB0E93BB7701694D07D1E5574E3AF937834*simid_608001691274051758*thid_OIP.AjUy2v!_4qvJNPUDkrG859QHaE2&vt=0&sim=11&iss=VSI&ajaxhist=0
35	https://www.theverge.com/2013/11/1/5054396/lockheed-martin-working-on-successor-to-legendary-sr-71-spy-plane
36	https://www.bing.com/images/search?view=detailV2&ccid=xQL8owVB&id=238BA701F17AD4392AAF4E58CCDA8EBFC46084BF&thid=OIP.xQL8owVB7BQMbaTie0iNrgHaJ4&mediaurl=https%3a%2f%2fc2.staticflickr.com%2f4%2f3169%2f2814621779_ebaf99b017_z.jpg&exph=640&expw=480&q=images+tires+and+landing+gear+for+sr-71&simid=608051237996268308&ck=1FB607CC2B94B7464B6A1A555B688C10&selectedIndex=31&qpvt=images+tires+and+landing+gear+for+sr-71&FORM=IRPRST&ajaxhist=0
37	https://www.bing.com/images/search?view=detailV2&ccid=IMjWjrxF&id=DA72C17CBCBDBF9AA493CC62FEBF8C355CEA736C&thid=OIP.IMjWjrxFhRwNDTz7t4becgHaE8&mediaurl=https%3a%2f%2ftheaviationgeekclub.com%2fwp-content%2fuploads%2f2019%2f05%2fBlackbird-Tire.jpg&exph=600&expw=900&q=image+sr+71+tires&simid=608027276309954587&ck=6D59663962D9D617A1DFBCF6822DED64&selectedIndex=4&qpvt=image+sr+71+tires&FORM=IRPRST&ajaxhist=0
38	http://www.wvi.com/~sr71webmaster/sr_sensors_pg1.htm
39	https://www.bing.com/images/search?view=detailV2&ccid=7GsHnIUZ&id=09A0D3AF4F2B29CDACA1832EE84597E491ECAEF5&thid=OIP.7GsHnIUZR5wZqGFcq-cTIQHaFH&mediaurl=https%3a%2f%2fphotorumors.com%2fwp-content%2fuploads%2f2012%2f01%2fPerkin-Elmer-36-F4.0-aerial-camera-lens2.png&exph=343&expw=496&q=image+perkin-elmer+camera+for+sr+71&simid=608002606077248197&ck=6EF2A82E7BCD2667A9705A7108E49B61&selectedIndex=14&qpvt=image+perkin-elmer+camera+for+sr+71&FORM=IRPRST&ajaxhist=0
40	http://www.wvi.com/~sr71webmaster/sr_sensors_pg1.htm
41	http://ambivalentengineer.blogspot.com/2013/04/optical-bar-cameras.html?m=1
42	https://en.wikipedia.org/wiki/Itek
43	https://nationalinterest.org/blog/buzz/1-infographic-proves-why-sr-71-spy-plane-was-simply-unbeatable-67642
44	https://www.bing.com/images/search?view=detailV2&ccid=H0riubpK&id=CB31B7D8EE69E815D791BBC88FE0D3B99899977C&thid=OIP.H0riubpKDnEpomBlrXg0HwHaE9&mediaurl=http%3A%2F%2Ffarm3.staticflickr.com%2F2134%2F2140071776_d0f2731846_z.jpg&exph=428&expw=639&q=image+camera+later+optical+bar+for+sr-71&simid=607994449916920718&ck=B37B4C263E65ECE305C7FC0D5F66E2E0&selectedindex=0&form=IRPRST&ajaxhist=0&vt=0&sim=11
45	https://www.456fis.org/SR-71_INSIDE_STORY.htm

#	References and Locations
46	https://en.citizendium.org/wiki/SR-71_Blackbird#Stealth
47	https://www.bing.com/images/search?view=detailV2&ccid=ZivZkJHw&id=4F3239524097694F9B866AB245F470265C16B57D&thid=OIP.ZivZkJHwj7yZtZEpCD5K8QHaE6&mediaurl=https%3A%2F%2Fi.stack.imgur.com%2FMOXd7.jpg&exph=421&expw=635&q=sr-71+teoc+camera+has+a+six+inch+resolution&simid=608015357864708788&ck=FAAB01027793A4C956C44D73CB823CAA&selectedindex=1&qpvt=sr-71+teoc+camera+has+a+six+inch+resolution&form=IRPRST&ajaxhist=0&vt=0&sim=11
48	http://iliketowastemytime.com/facts-you-didnt-know-about-sr71-blackbird
49	https://www.thedrive.com/the-war-zone/17207/sr-71s-r2-d2-could-be-the-key-to-winning-future-fights-in-gps-denied-environments
50	https://www.bing.com/images/search?view=detailV2&ccid=w90jvCx%2b&id=DDE66D0D3EB44E15D4E5161B1136C694D33E45CD&thid=OIP.w90jvCx-_gxsJ69zzcPnMgHaG8&mediaurl=http%3a%2f%2fupload.wikimedia.org%2fwikipedia%2fcommons%2fc%2fc2%2fc%2fCorona_spysat_camera_system.jpg&exph=519&expw=553&q=images+camera+schematic+nose+sr-71&simid=608025446718769362&ck=C93EF68232ADB902A9A0E5A395317231&selectedIndex=28&qpvt=images+camera+schematic+nose+sr-71&FORM=IRPRST&ajaxhist=0
51	https://www.bing.com/images/search?view=detailV2&ccid=2%2f%2fVNrJ2&id=BAA51719D63BA91623A6815F22548E37C5D4C423&thid=OIP.2__VNrJ2KBIY7wMTSBcRwQHaEo&mediaurl=https%3a%2f%2fi.redd.it%2f2fqi91l7urzja01.png&exph=1600&expw=2560&q=image+radar+setup+nose+sr+71&simid=608000909558418233&ck=BCD9305985129136D8DF692AA6017389&selectedIndex=0&FORM=IRPRST&ajaxhist=0
52	https://www.thedrive.com/the-war-zone/29787/the-sr-71-blackbirds-predecessor-created-plasma-stealth-by-burning-cesium-laced-fuel
53	https://en.wikipedia.org/wiki/JP-7
54	http://www.roadrunnersinternationale.com/articles/rcs_5.jpg
55	https://www.amazon.com/Sled-Driver-Flying-Worlds-Fastest/dp/0929823087/ref=sr_1_1?crid=3U2RCZCCB5OX2&dchild=1&keywords=sled+driver+brian+shul&qid=1605709714&s=books&sprefix=sled+driver+brains%2Cstripbooks%2C155&sr=1-1
56	http://www.sr-71.org/blackbird/
57	https://www.bing.com/images/search?view=detailV2&ccid=Il4n0HFg&id=4FA47F9F5742BC733B7EA8CCEC696179CE507CFC&thid=OIP.Il4n0HFgjKGn1lDgiCuBmgHaD9&mediaurl=https%3a%2f%2fi.pinimg.com%2f736x%2f90%2ffd%2f93%2f90fd9384eb3e95a4bf9d375472137816--the-secret-blackbird.jpg&exph=394&expw=736&q=image+was+yf-12+single+seater&simid=607995051179051458&ck=74843C11A7206EF4623D2932AADEB532&selectedIndex=0&qpvt=image+was+yf-12+single+seater&FORM=IRPRST&ajaxhist=0
58	https://www.bing.com/images/search?view=detailV2&ccid=r1MuxQxB&id=3CFC5AE19390D484B1BA9635E77E2DC6C45C86A2&thid=OIP.r1MuxQxBJAOv-WiiTBD4SgHaF8&mediaurl=https%3a%2f%2fairandspace.si.edu%2fsites%2fdefault%2ffiles%2f2fimages%2fcollection-objects%2frecord-images%2fNASM-SI-71-2946.jpg&exph=1607&expw=2000&q=image+yf+12+aircraft&simid=607989703896861049&ck=A8365865C354EBAAE65F44C7D181677A&selectedIndex=0&qpvt=image+yf+12+aircraft&FORM=IRPRST&ajaxhist=0
59	https://aviationhumor.net/why-is-sr-71-blackbird-an-aircraft-like-no-other/
60	https://www.reddit.com/r/aviation/comments/bg0as0/cia_a12_oxcart_vs_usaf_sr71_blackbird_whats_the/
61	https://taskandpurpose.com/military-tech/sr-71-blackbird-afterburners-photos/
62	https://www.bing.com/images/search?view=detailV2&ccid=WCKIrimW&id=8F3EA91D294ADA119C5C9522854A4BA273CD5BAC&thid=OIP.WCKIrimWMxJsh0TcrS9GbQHaCv&mediaurl=https%3a%2f%2fqph.fs.quoracdn.net%2fmain-qimg-ef5db860b4833e59832e8a5d67d6276e-c&exph=223&expw=602&q=image+sr+71+vs+a12&simid=608039834825786261&ck=2B10574F0242160A2A4FB6A996684D86&selectedIndex=0&qpvt=image+sr+71+vs+a12&FORM=IRPRST&ajaxhist=0
63	https://foreignpolicy.com/slideshow/drones-a-photo-history/

#	References and Locations
64	http://www.grissomairmuseum.com/gallery/drones/plane-27
65	https://en.wikipedia.org/wiki/Lockheed_D-21#/media/File:M-21_Rear.jpg
66	https://www.amazon.com/Projects-Skunk-Works-Lockheed-Development/dp/0760350329/ref=tmm_hrd_swatch_0?_encoding=UTF8&qid=1605710494&sr=1-1
67	https://www.cia.gov/library/center-for-the-study-of-intelligence/kent-csi/vol15no1/html/v15i1a01p_0001.htm
68	http://www.lockheedmartin.com/us/100years/stories/blackbird.html
69	https://www.lockheedmartin.com/en-us/news/features/history/blackbird.html
70	https://en.wikipedia.org/wiki/Kelly_Johnson_(engineer)
71	https://theavgeeks.com/2020/05/03/long-read-the-oxcart-story/
72	https://www.bing.com/images/search?view=detailV2&ccid=HWgXiAE%2f&id=97FA50FE626CF1F0B9CECA793132635E8BAD55CA&thid=OIP.HWgXiAE_Mo-XJ6lVxjSSYQHaFr&mediaurl=https%3a%2f%2fth.bing.com%2fth%2fid%2fR1d681788013f328f9727a215c6349261%3frik%3dylWti15jMjF5yg%26riu%3dhttp%253a%252f%252fwww.wvi.com%252f%25257Esr71webmaster%252fkelly102.jpg%26ehk%3dTQ6D2pC1lPGs7m3i6xsX%252fkXTU8rd2jBSj7aoGKf7mv4%253d%26risl%3d%26pid%3dlmgRaw&exph=368&expw=480&q=images+kelly+johnson+of+lockheed&simid=608009589755872145&ck=00587156DB0E49DED4354171C8807DE6&selectedIndex=18&qpvt=images+kelly+johnson+of+lockheed&FORM=IRPRST&ajaxhist=0
73	https://www.bing.com/images/search?view=detailV2&ccid=nRBg%2b8gR&id=FBF845E1248A506059EDEE7A725C9BA9251F2DC0&thid=OIP.nRBg-8gRm5vk3lOgBHuGKQHaEH&mediaurl=https%3a%2f%2fth.bing.com%2fth%2fid%2fR9d1060fbc8119b9be4de53a0047b8629%3frik%3dwC0fJambXHJ67g%26riu%3dhttp%253a%252f%252fwww.quartoknows.com%252fblog%252fquartoexplores%252fwp-content%252fuploads%252fsites%252f5%252f2015%252f10%252fSR-71-1a12.jpg%26ehk%3dQ%252floDdMfx4McPdzhp3SPkHwkTY1zrt2naDjOHNDbsMc%253d%26risl%3d%26pid%3dlmgRaw&exph=447&expw=803&q=images+kelly+johnson+of+lockheed&simid=607993801419721885&ck=487238B7AB3F5102F05E7CF301FF073D&selectedIndex=19&qpvt=images+kelly+johnson+of+lockheed&FORM=IRPRST&ajaxhist=0
74	https://www.bing.com/images/search?view=detailV2&ccid=e8j5o9Ad&id=DE575E26864239E5D83405D686277849E4C262E7&thid=OIP.e8j5o9AdT5dmFbVuVLGTYwHaE2&mediaurl=https%3a%2f%2fi.stack.imgur.com%2fxXyLF.jpg&exph=1048&expw=1600&q=image+external+nose++sr+-+71&simid=607990434096351573&ck=4841B029DB4038BA148B52A8FB965B25&selectedIndex=8&FORM=IRPRST&ajaxhist=0
75	https://content.satimagingcorp.com/static/galleryimages/ikonos-area-51.jpg
76	https://www.bing.com/images/search?view=detailV2&ccid=HZ4lXeyV&id=549E653766D50E1159090825CD59E6EAAEEFC27D&thid=OIP.HZ4lXeyV7uaHsQGP9pjYDwHaFe&mediaurl=https%3A%2F%2Fwww.cia.gov%2Fnews-information%2Ffeatured-story-archive%2F2015-featured-story-archive%2Fimages%2Farea-51%2FHousing-at-Watertown.jpg%2Fimage.jpg&exph=666&expw=900&q=roadrunners+internationale+trailers+area+51&simid=608031652906272705&ck=1299823D7CD82C3C66133D3BFA2A5EE5&selectedindex=1&qpvt=roadrunners+internationale+trailers+area+51&form=IRPRST&ajaxhist=0&vt=0&sim=11
77	https://www.bing.com/images/search?view=detailV2&ccid=sSHF9sUQ&id=3882A2BDEF9FEF88B00317E55F933C90F34565C1&thid=OIP.sSHF9sUQY0D8rzKmgBOYDAHaEg&mediaurl=http%3a%2f%2fstatic.lakana.com%2fnxsglobal%2flasvegasnow%2fphoto%2f2017%2f08%2f23%2f957construction_1503529018078_25390106_ver1.0.jpg&exph=2298&expw=3774&q=image%2357+lockheed+build+number+-+2008+under+construction+at+lockheed%27s+plant+in+burbank%2c+california.&simid=608020374189834358&ck=F3F42D34FA5CBC9F2B6E9C69623FBE5E&selectedIndex=0&FORM=IRPRST&ajaxhist=0
78	http://roadrunnersinternationale.com/transporting_the_a-12.html

#	References and Locations
79	http://www.habu.org/photogallery.html
80	http://www.sr-71.org/blackbird/manual/1/1-22.php
81	http://www.dfrc.nasa.gov/Gallery/Photo/SR-71/HTML/EC96-43463-1.html
82	https://theaviationist.com/2013/12/04/sr-71-speed-enemy/
83	https://www.bing.com/images/search?view=detailV2&ccid=QH925Ovs&id=7B2E0FA6EA3138 0686DBA17B8A8CC9BC4078CA21&thid=OIP.QH925OvsvvMTJrkbq9ZgowHaJu&mediaurl=htt ps%3a%2f%2fi.pinimg.com%2foriginals%2f68%2f61%2f49%2f686149bd9a3851b964a08576fd 8e6729.jpg&exph=2695&expw=2053&q=images+area+51+groom+lake+airport+aerial+view&s imid=608021044291961359&ck=BAFE059B108CEA4D8C7B36FABBAC4AD4&selectedIndex=0 &FORM=IRPRST&ajaxhist=0
84	https://www.sr-71.org/groomlake/2004/index.php?file=warningsigns-2004-01.jpg
85	https://military.wikia.org/wiki/Lockheed_A-12?file=A12radartesting.jpg
86	https://www.bing.com/images/search?view=detailV2&ccid=%2bNsl7fod&id=1B308FC016241 F30A2D9C5B833207734C2F09F1C&thid=OIP.-Nsl7fodMN0pjYMI_5xxjQHaE8&mediaurl=https%3a%2f%2f1.bp.blogspot.com%2f-NZOv4VOT-cY%2fXdHiKbYRszI%2fAAAAAAAAYVU%2fT_cUpFi7HcsCy-KzRc5lWjU44E1_MOB9QCLcBGAsYHQ%2fs1600%2fUSAF%252B9068%252BMemorial%252 BMt.%252BCharleston.JPG&exph=1067&expw=1600&q=cold+war+memorial+at+the+base+of +mount+charleston+area+51&simid=608011556831889382&ck=A474FD74E50B237AD9A2465 BD582D833&selectedIndex=9&qpvt=cold+war+memorial+at+the+base+of+mount+charleston +area+51&FORM=IRPRST&ajaxhist=0
87	https://www.bing.com/images/search?view=detailV2&ccid=%2fHSj5W9k&id=70894BB59DA3 952A6A0443106BF17D48893648AC&thid=OIP._HSj5W9k6nJKYFjsk8KcdgHaFS&mediaurl=htt ps%3a%2f%2fi1.wp.com%2ftheavgeeks.com%2fwp-content%2fuploads%2f2019%2f07%2fOXCART-Fleet-1964-A-12-SR-71.jpg%3fw%3d1400%26ssl%3d1&exph=706&expw=990&q=images+the+'oxcart'+"+fleet+in+ 1964&simid=608019691357276769&ck=03EB214ED7F891E28B2DE076CD08D121&selectedIn dex=0&qpvt=images+the+'oxcart+"+fleet+in+1964&FORM=IRPRST&ajaxhist=0
88	https://www.cia.gov/library/center-for-the-study-of-intelligence/csi-publications/books-and-monographs/a-12/finding-a-mission.html
89	CIA Library - McCone memorandum for the record, "Discussion at NSC Meeting—5 May 1964," 5 May 1964.
90	CIA Library - Carter memorandum to Wheelon, "SKYLARK," 22 August 1964.
91	CIA Library - [DS&T,] "Vulnerability of the OXCART Vehicle to the Cuban Air Defense System," 15 September 1964; NRO Acting Director memorandum to Deputy Undersecretary of State for Political Affairs et al., "OXCART Reconnaissance of Cuba," 6 September 1966; Peter Jessup (NSC) memorandum, "Minutes of the Meeting of the 303 Committee, 15 September 1966," 16 September 1966; Wheelon to McCone, "Considerations bearing on OXCART use over Cuba," 7 September 1966; CIA Board of National Estimates to Helms, "Probable Communist Reactions to Use of the OXCART for Reconnaissance over Cuba," 6 September 1966; Pedlow and Welzenbach, 44.
92	CIA Library - Raborn, "Memorandum For the President," 20 August 1965.
93	CIA Library - CIA Director of Special Activities to CIA Director of Reconnaissance, "Operational Readiness of the OXCART System," 12 November 1965; McIninch, 23.
94	CIA Library - Board of National Estimates, "Political Problems Involved in Operating OXCART Missions from Okinawa over Communist China and North Vietnam," 29 November 1965.
95	CIA Library - Peter Jessup (NSC) memorandum for the President, "Proposed Deployment and Use of A-12 Aircraft," 11 April 1966; Raborn memorandum to the President, "OXCART Deployment Proposal," 29 April 1966; Raborn memorandum to the 303 Committee, "OXCART Deployment," 15 June 1966; Special National Intelligence Estimate 10-2-66, "Reactions to a Possible US Course of Action," 17 March 1966; "OXCART Development Summary and Progress (1 October 1966-31 December 1966)."

#	References and Locations
96	CIA Library - [OSA,] "Briefing Note for the Director of Central Intelligence...OXCART Status Report," 15 February 1967
97	CIA Library - Helms memorandum to the 303 Committee, "OXCART Reconnaissance of North Vietnam," with attachment, 15 May 1967.
98	https://www.bing.com/images/search?view=detailV2&ccid=GddSt%2FRm&id=DDE64AEADC 2E250CE7BE5EC298D5FA3BA5B7876A&thid=OIP.GddSt_RmCGb_YanhY5hMBgHaFR&media url=https%3A%2F%2Fupload.wikimedia.org%2Fwikipedia%2Fcommons%2F8%2F81%2FHan oi_1967.jpg&exph=499&expw=700&q=image+of+the+hanoi+area%2c+taken+during+the+four th+mission%2c+in+june+1967&simid=608040109718113724&ck=2514533CADF2565214B51C 141C4A373C&selectedindex=0&qpvt=image+of+the+hanoi+area%2c+taken+during+the+four th+mission%2c+in+june+1967&form=IRPRST&ajaxhist=0&vt=0&sim=11
99	CIA Library - [OSA,] "Critique for OXCART Mission BSX001," 6 June 1967; DS&T, "BLACK SHIELD Reconnaissance Missions, 31 May-15 August 1967," 22 September 1967, 3-4; National Photographic Interpretation Center (NPIC), "BLACK SHIELD Mission X-001, 31 May 1967," NPIC/R-112/67, June 1967; [OSA,] "Critique for OXCART Mission Number BX6705," 26 June 1967, and "Critique for OXCART Mission Number BX6732," 3 November 1967.
100	CIA Library - OSA mission critiques, 16 June 1967-15 May 1968; DS&T, "BLACK SHIELD Reconnaissance Missions, 16 August-31 December 1967," 31 January 1968, and "BLACKSHIELD Reconnaissance Missions, 1 January-31 March 1968."
101	CIA Library - Quoted in Rich and Janos, 244.
102	CIA Library - DS&T, "BLACK SHIELD Reconnaissance Missions, 16 August-31 December 1967," 31 January 1968, 18-22; D/OSA memorandum to DDS&T, "Analysis of Surface to Air Missile Engagements for OXCART Missions BX6732 and BX6734," 27 November 1967.
103	CIA Library - DDS&T Carl Duckett memorandum to DCI Richard Helms, "OXCART Operations on 27, 28, 29 October (local time)"; DS&T, "BLACK SHIELD Reconnaissance Missions, 16 August-31 December 1967," 31 January 1968, 25-35; D/OSA memorandum to DDS&T, "Analysis of Surface to Air Missile Engagements for OXCART Missions BX6732 and BX6734," 27 November 1967; Cable OPCEN 2898, 30 October 1967; Cable from Kadena, IN 91487, 1 November 1967; Donald Smith (EA/DDCI) untitled memorandum to Duckett, 6 November 1967.
104	https://en.m.wikipedia.org/wiki/USS_Pueblo_%28AGER-2%29
105	CIA Library - Quoted in Rich and Janos, 245.
106	CIA Library - NPIC, "North Korea Mission BX 6847, 26 January 1968, Highlights," NPIC/R-17/68, January 1968; DS&T, "BLACK SHIELD Reconnaissance Missions, 1 January-31 March 1968," 30 April 1968, 8-10.
107	CIA Library - Joseph F. Carroll (Director, DIA) memorandum to Chairman, Joint Chiefs of Staff, "Requirement for a Second BLACK SHIELD Mission Over North Korea," 29 January 1968; "Report on Meeting of the [Pueblo] Advisory Group" and "Notes of the President's Luncheon Meeting with Senior American Advisors," both 29 January 1968, FRUS, XXIX, Part 1, 557, 565; DS&T, "BLACK SHIELD Reconnaissance Missions, 1 January-31 March 1968," 30 April 1968, 11, and "BLACK SHIELD Reconnaissance Missions, 1 April-9 June 1968," 7 August 1968, 2-3; CIA Intelligence Information Cable, "Implications of Reported Relocation of USS Pueblo," 12 February 1968, Declassified Documents Reference System, doc. no. CK3100137943.
108	Book - SR-71 Revealed https://www.amazon.com/SR-71-Revealed-Richard-H-Graham/dp/0760301220/ref=sr_1_1?dchild=1&keywords=Book+-+SR-71+Revealed&qid=1608485798&sr=8-1
109	http://drco.pairserver.com/manuals/LOCKHEED%20SR71.pdf
110	http://roadrunnersinternationale.com/pw_tales.htm
111	Kloesel, Kurt J.; Ratnayake, Nalin A.; Clark, Casie M. "A Technology Pathway for Airbreathing, Combined-Cycle, Horizontal Space Launch Through SR-71 Based Trajectory Modeling" (PDF). Dryden Flight Research Center. NASA. Retrieved 7 September 2011.
112	"The Engines of Pratt & Whitney: A Technical History" Jack Connors, ISBN 978-1-60086-711-8

194

#	References and Locations
113	"Factsheets: Pratt & Whitney J58 TurboJet". National Museum of the Air Force.
114	"A Look at the Pratt & Whitney J-58JT11D-20". Copyright © 2014 Atomic Toasters.
115	"Martin P6M Seamaster". The Aviation History On-Line Museum. Created April 12, 1997. Updated November 2, 2013.
116	Goodall, James and Jay Miller. "Lockheed's SR-71 ':' Family A-12, F-12, M-21, D-21, SR-71". Hinckley, England: AeroFax-Midland Publishing, 2002. ISBN 1-85780-138-5
117	http://materiales.azc.uam.mx/gjl/Clases/MA10_I/Roark's%20formulas%20for%20stress%20and%20strain.pdf
118	https://militarymachine.com/wp-content/uploads/2018/08/Keuffel__Esser_slide_rule_model_4081-3_ca._1940_-_Detail.jpg
119	https://caveviews.blogs.com/cave_news/2018/06/when-was-the-last-time-you-saw-a-freiden-manual-rotary-calculator.html
120	https://en.wikipedia.org/wiki/IBM_700/7000_series#/media/File:IBM_Electronic_Data_Processing_Machine_-_GPN-2000-001881.jpg
121	http://www.dtic.mil/dtic/tr/fulltext/u2/a107863.pdf
122	https://en.wikipedia.org/wiki/Photoelasticity#:~:text=Photoelastic%20experiments%20%28also%20informally%20referred%20to%20as%20photoelasticity%29,used%20for%20determining%20stress%20concentration%20in%20irregular%20geometries.
123	http://www.enginehistory.org/Convention/2013/SR-71PropulsionSystem-2013.pdf
124	"Jet Propulsion for Aerospace Applications" Second Edition, Walter J. Hesse Nicholas V.S. Mumford Pitman Publishing Corporation 1964 Fig 14.7 "Compressor performance map showing effect of flight Mach number on operating points"
125	U.S. Patent 3,344,606, "Recover Bleed Air Turbojet," Robert B. Abernethy
126	https://en.wikipedia.org/wiki/Pratt_%26_Whitney_J58
127	http://arc.uta.edu/publications/cp_files/AIAA%202003-0185.pdf
128	"SR-71 Revealed "Richard H.Graham,Col USAF(Retd) ISBN 978-0-7603-0122-7 p46
129	"The Engine of Pratt & Whitney: A Technical History"Jack Connors ISBN 9781-60086-711-8 p325 J58 compressor map showing the take-off operating point
130	https://www.thesr71blackbird.com/Aircraft/Engines/j58-the-powerplant-for-the-blackbirds
131	https://en.wikipedia.org/wiki/Pratt_%26_Whitney_J58#Materials
132	https://www.enginehistory.org/members/Convention/2014/Presentations/SR-71InletDesign.pdf
133	https://www.bing.com/images/search?view=detailV2&ccid=4ggwz%2f9Y&id=8ABCF88B394A28F70CB637A9E2A8109A63CC0574&thid=OIP.4ggwz_9YazWajieUdnc3PAHaE9&mediaurl=http%3a%2f%2fwww.wvi.com%2f%7cesr71webmaster%2fyf12inl.gif&exph=413&expw=616&q=close-up+with+inlet+spike+installed+with+"Mice"++sr+71&simid=608027692908741570&ck=705FEEE3803DF31E942082E3ABE914CC&selectedIndex=0&FORM=IRPRST&ajaxhist=0
134	http://drco.pairserver.com/manuals/LOCKHEED%20SR71.pdf
135	https://www.colorado.edu/faculty/kantha/sites/default/files/attached-files/russell.pdf
136	http://www.worldlibrary.org/articles/eng/j-58
137	https://www.bing.com/images/search?view=detailV2&ccid=BG1n4EU5&id=0A0352038BB6234DDB4A1D4221303E796B6BE61E&thid=OIP.BG1n4EU58SrpfPKKOnUASQAAAA&mediaurl=https%3a%2f%2fqph.fs.quoracdn.net%2fmain-qimg-6f6190ea301955a1c4cb045204a78d3-c&exph=500&expw=412&q=image+schematic+SR-71+Engine+Design&simid=608016590521697909&ck=E8BD81ACDB63EF6DB77B8F397F744C85&selectedIndex=37&FORM=IRPRST&ajaxhist=0
138	http://enginehistory.org/GasTurbines/P&W/J58/J58.shtml
139	"History of Thermal barrier Coatings for Gas Turbine Engines emphasizing NASA's role from 1942 to 1990" Robert A. Miller, NASA TM 2009-215459
140	https://patents.google.com/patent/US20150121884A1/en?q=keykole+slots+gas+turbine&oq=keykole+slots++gas+turbine

#	References and Locations
141	http://aerostories.free.fr/technique/J58/J58_01/page11.html
142	https://www.bing.com/images/search?view=detailV2&ccid=g0dBxh2C&id=C1A9F9E7337104B4C431BBA1693653AFB1E51F22&thid=OIP.g0dBxh2Cb8xVZTY8GltZbQHaFj&mediaurl=https%3a%2f%2fs-media-cache-ak0.pinimg.com%2foriginals%2f21%2f50%2f5b%2f21505bfc7f24d7f26a03589f8ec02411.jpg&cdnurl=https%3a%2f%2fth.bing.com%2fth%2fid%2fR.834741c61d826fcc5565363c1a5b596d%3frik%3dlh%252flsa9TNmmhuw%26pid%3dImgRaw%2r%3d0&exph=2112&expw=2816&q=images+J58+gas+turbine&simid=608023814304780489&FORM=IRPRST&ck=0B27F6AC917D81ADCAB54245FA41B902&selectedIndex=0&ajaxhist=0&ajaxserp=0
143	https://www.cambridge.org/core/journals/aeronautical-journal/article/abs/buckling-at-high-temperature/BC3F0C001DE7C94639DC8BA344CCD5C6
144	https://en.wikipedia.org/wiki/JP-7
145	https://en.wikipedia.org/wiki/Triethylborane
146	https://weaponsandwarfare.com/2020/01/10/a-12-operational/
147	https://www.scribd.com/document/530130579/An-Introduction-to-the-Design-and-Behavior-of-Bolted-Joints-Third-Edition-Revised-and-Expanded-PDFDrive
148	Patent # 4841725 by Excello Corp. Fuel Spray Device
149	http://aerostories.free.fr/technique/J58/J58_01/page12.html
150	https://www.amazon.com/SR-71-Revealed-Richard-H-Graham/dp/0760301220/ref=sr_1_1?keywords=sr-71+revealed+graham&qid=1638388398&sr=8-1
151	https://wisconsinmetaltech.com/titanium-and-the-sr-71/
152	https://en.wikipedia.org/wiki/Northrop_Grumman_RQ-180
153	https://www.sr-71.org/blackbird/locations.php
154	https://revolyution.wordpress.com/2015/08/05/kelly-johnsons-14-rules/#:~:text=%20Kelly%20Johnson's%2014%20Rules%20%201%20The,restricted%20in%20an%20almost%20vicious%20manner.%20More%20
155	https://roadrunnersinternationale.com/sr-71timeline.pdf
156	https://www.thedrive.com/the-war-zone/32788/the-sr-71-blackbird-was-almost-brought-back-for-the-global-war-on-terror#:~:text=Proponents%20of%20the%20Blackbird%20believed%20a%20mistake%20had,the%20SR-71%20was%20a%20hard%20program%20to%20kill.
157	https://en.wikipedia.org/wiki/Lockheed_A-12
158	http://starlanevineyard.com/our-story/history-of-the-vineyard/
159	https://en.wikipedia.org/wiki/Concorde
160	https://militarymachine.com/sr-71-facts/
161	https://www.thedrive.com/the-war-zone/32722/cias-predecessor-to-the-sr-71-blackbird-tested-electron-guns-to-hide-from-radars
162	https://duckduckgo.com/?q=images+Lockheed+CL-+400+Design+For++%22Suntan%22+&t=h_&iar=images&iax=images&ia=images&iai=https%3A%2F%2Fweaponsandwarfare.files.wordpress.com%2F2020%2F05%2Fejtyu.jpg%3Fw%3D500
163	https://en.wikipedia.org/wiki/Lockheed_Martin_SR-72
164	https://en.wikipedia.org/wiki/Northrop_Grumman_RQ-180
165	https://science.howstuffworks.com/satellite10.htm

More Reading Material

#	Book	Author	Paperback Price on Amazon
1	Speed - The life of a Test Pilot and Birth of an American Icon	Bob Gilliland	$3.11
2	The Complete Book of the SR-71 Blackbird: The Illustrated Profile of Every Aircraft, Crew, and Breakthrough of the World's Fastest Stealth Jet	Richard Graham	$49.12
3	Lockheed SR-71 Blackbird: The Illustrated History of America's Legendary Mach 3 Spy Plane	James C Goodall	$39.99
4	SR-71 Blackbird: Stories, Tales, and Legends	Richard Graham	$26.70
5	Kelly: More Than My Share of It All	Kelly Johnson	$21.95
6	SR-71 Flight Manual: The Official Pilot's Handbook Declassified and Expanded with Commentary	Richard Graham	$38.45
7	Skunk Works: A Personal Memoir of My Years at Lockheed	Ben Rich	$14.29
8	SR-71: The Complete Illustrated History of the Blackbird, The World's Highest, Fastest Plane	Richard Graham	$16.49
9	Secret Jets: A History of the Aircraft Developed At Area 51	Bill Yenne	$14.89
10	From Rainbow to Gusto: Stealth and the Design of the Lockheed Blackbird	Paul Schuler	$39.95
11	Flying the SR-71 Blackbird: In the Cockpit on a Secret Operational Mission	Richard Graham	$18.75
12	SR-71, the Blackbird, Q&A	Terry Pappas	$31.39
13	Lockheed SR-71 Operations in Europe and the Middle East	Paul Crickmore	$24.00